D1223809

Out of Sight

Other Books by Eamon Grennan

Poetry

What Light There Is & Other Poems
As If It Matters
So It Goes
Relations: New & Selected Poems
Still Life with Waterfall
The Quick of It
Matter of Fact

Translation

Leopardi: Selected Poems
Oedipus at Colonus (with Rachel Kitzinger)

Essays

Facing the Music: Irish Poetry in the Twentieth Century

Out of Sight

New & Selected Poems

Eamon Grennan

GRAYWOLF PRESS

With the exception of the *New Poems* (2006–2008) section, almost all of the poems in the present collection also appeared in the following editions from The Gallery Press in Ireland: *Wildly for Days* (1983), *What Light There Is* (1987), *As If It Matters* (1991), *So It Goes* (1995), *Selected and New Poems* (2000), *Still Life with Waterfall* (2001), *The Quick of It* (2004), and *Out of Breath* (2007). For this, the author thanks Peter Fallon.

This publication is made possible by funding provided in part by a grant from the Minnesota State Arts Board, through an appropriation by the Minnesota State Legislature, a grant from the National Endowment for the Arts, and private funders. Significant support has also been provided by Target; the McKnight Foundation; and other generous contributions from foundations, corporations, and individuals. To these organizations and individuals we offer our heartfelt thanks.

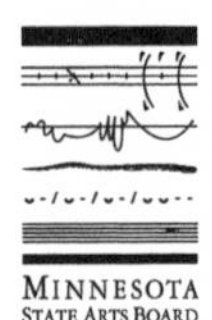

Published by Graywolf Press
250 Third Avenue North, Suite 600
Minneapolis, Minnesota 55401

www.graywolfpress.org

Published in the United States of America

ISBN 978-1-55597-564-7

2 4 6 8 9 7 5 3 1
First Graywolf Printing, 2010

Library of Congress Control Number: 2010920771

Cover design: Jeenee Lee Design

Cover art: Mark Rothko, *Untitled (Violet, Black, Orange, Yellow on White and Red),* 1949. Oil on canvas. 81½ x 66 inches (207 x 167.6 cm). Solomon R. Guggenheim Museum, New York. Gift, Elaine and Werner Dannheisser and The Dannheisser Foundation, 1978. 78.2461. © 1998 Kate Rothko Prizel and Christopher Rothko / Artists Rights Society (ARS), New York.

for Rachel

Contents

FROM *The Quick of It* 2005

FROM *Matter of Fact* 2008

Slanting Pillars of Light, like Ladders up to Heaven, their base always a field of vivid green Sunshine . . . The Lake has been a Mirror so very clear, that the Water became almost invisible—and now it rolls in white Breakers like a Sea; and the Wind snatches up the Water, and drifts it like Snow. —And now the Rain Storm pelts against my Study Window!

—SAMUEL TAYLOR COLERIDGE
Notebooks: Wednesday morning, October 19, 1803

FROM *What Light There Is & Other Poems* 1989

Facts of Life, Ballymoney

I would like to let things be:

The rain comes down on the roof
The small birds come to the feeder
The waves come slowly up the strand.

Three sounds to measure
My hour here at the window:
The slow swish of the sea
The squeak of hungry birds
The quick ticking of rain.

Then of course there are the trees—
Bare for the most part.
The grass wide open to the rain
Clouds accumulating over the sea
The water rising and falling and rising
Herring-gulls bobbing on the water.

They are killing cuttlefish out there,
One at a time without fuss.
With a brisk little shake of the head
They rinse their lethal beaks.

Rain-swollen, the small stream
Twists between slippery rocks.
That's all there's to it, spilling
Its own sound onto the sand.

In one breath one wink all this
Melts to an element in my blood.
And still it's possible to go on
Simply living
As if nothing had happened.

Nothing has happened:
Rain inching down the window,
Me looking out at the rain.

A Gentle Art

(for my mother)

I've been learning how to light a fire
Again, after thirty years. Begin (she'd say)
With a bed of yesterday's newspapers—
Disasters, weddings, births and deaths,
All that everyday black and white of
History is first to go up in smoke. The sticks
Crosswise, holding in their dry heads
Memories of detonating blossom, leaf. Saved
From the ashes of last night's fire,
Arrange the cinders among the sticks:
Crown them with coal nuggets, handling
Such antiquity as behooves it,
For out of this darkness, light. Look,
It's a cold but comely thing
I've put together as my mother showed me,
Down to sweeping the fireplace clean. Lit,
You must cover from view, let it concentrate—
Some things being better done in secret.
Pretend another interest, but never
Let it slip your mind: know its breathing,
Its gulps and little gasps, its silence
And satisfied whispers, its lapping air.
At a certain moment you may be sure (she'd say)
It's caught. Then you simply leave it be:
It's on its own now, leading its mysterious
Hungry life, becoming more itself by the minute,
Like a child grown up, growing strange.

Swifts over Dublin

Stop, look up, and welcome these
Artful dodgers, high-flyers on the wing,
These ecstatic swirlers, sons of air
And daring, daughters of the slow burn,
Who twist and kiss and veer, high
As kites on homecoming. Survivors,

They've put their night-sweats by,
Harrowing darkness in a rumour of wings
And companionable squeaking, riding the blast.
But now, how they celebrate a comeback, casting
High-pitched benedictions down
On shopping centres, stray dogs, monoxide traffic.

From any point of view
They are beyond me, dark sparks of mystery
I must look up to, where they usher
The full flush of summer in, highly
Delighted with themselves, and sporting
Their keen, seasonal dominion.

In the National Gallery, London

(for Derek Mahon)

These Dutchmen are in certain touch
With the world we walk on. Velvet
And solid as summer, their chestnut cows
Repeat cloud contours, lie of the land.

Everything gathers the light in its fashion:
That boat's ribbed bulging, the ripple
Of red tweed at the oarsman's shoulder,
the way wood displaces water, how water
Sheens still, the colour of pale irises.

How your eye enters this avenue
Of tall, green-tufted, spinal trees:
You tense to the knuckled ruts, nod
To the blunted huntsman and his dog,
A farmer tying vines, that discreet couple
Caught in conversation at a barn's brown angle.
You enter the fellowship of laundered light.

From the ritual conducted around this table
These men in black stare coolly back at you,
Their business, a wine contract, done with.
And on brightly polished ice these villagers

Are bound to one another by the bleak
Intimacies of winter light, a surface
Laid open like a book, where they flock—
Festive and desperate as birds of passage
Between seasons—knowing that enclosing sky
Like the back of their hands: at home
In the cold, making no bones of it.

Muse, Maybe

You are never at home with her.
Private, she shies the familiar touch.
Lady of half-lights,
You cannot make her out from shadows.

There's no catching up with her:
She sleeps near your sleep,
Your mind wears her face like a mask,
She is the lady of changes.

She's the girl you kissed in the graveyard,
Hers the warm skin under a raincoat.
You turned sixteen that winter, speechless
At heart, for all your speeches.

She wears the air of what's possible,
Making your pulse ache.
Find me out, she says,
Put me in the clear.

You've made such promises before.

End of Winter

I spent the morning my father died
Catching flies. They'd buzz and hum
Against the warm illuminated pane
Of the living-room window. Breathless,
My hand would butterfly behind them
And cup their fear in my fist,
Their filament wings tickling
The soft centre of my palm. With my
Left hand I unlatched the window
And opened my right wide in the sunshine.
They'd spin for a second like stunned
Ballerinas, then off with them, tiny
Hearts rattling like dice, recovered
From the fright of their lives. I watch
Each one spiral the astonishing
Green world of grass, drift
Between the grey branches of the ash.
I see each quick dark shadow
Smudge the rinsed and springing earth
That shone beyond belief all morning.
There must have been at least a dozen
I saved like that with my own hands
Through the morning, when they shook off sleep
In every corner of the living room.

Taking My Son to School

His first day. Waiting, he plays
By himself in the garden.
I take a photo he clowns for,
Catching him, as it were, in flight.

All the way there in the car he chatters
And sings, giving me directions.
There are no maps for this journey:
It is the wilderness we enter.

Around their tall, bespectacled teacher
A gaggle of young ones in summer colours:
Silent, he stands on their border
Clutching a bunch of purple dahlias.

Shyly, he offers them up to her—
Distracted, she holds them upside down.
He teeters on the rim of the circle,
Head drooping, a flower after rain.

I kiss him goodbye and leave him:
Stiff, he won't meet my eye.
I drive by him but he doesn't wave.
In my mind I rush to his rescue.

The distance bleeding between us,
I steal a last look back:
From a thicket of blondes, brunettes,
His red hair blazes.

It is done. I have handed him over.
I remember him wildly dancing—
Naked and shining, shining
In the empty garden.

At My Sister's Flat in London

Decent the white flowers on the table
Telling the exact centre—daisies,
Their bright eyes open wide—
And the table laid for breakfast:
The brown bread coupled to its knife
The butter golden in a green dish
Strong tea brewing in a blue pot
Orange juice brimming a shapely glass.

Things of the ordinary morning world:
This morning luminant under low cloud
Over the tilt solidity of roofs,
Their grey slates palely shining.
And in the misted distance the green
Encouraging curvature of trees.

You bless in your own abiding way
Civilities of the garden parcelled out
To tame grass and the dazzle of roses,
These shrill swifts scything the air,
Keeping their hearts up in every weather.

Lying Low

The dead rabbit's
Raspberry belly
Gapes like a mouth;

Bees and gilded flies
Make the pulpy flesh
Hum and squirm:

O love, they sing
In their nail-file voices,
We are becoming one another.

His head intact, tranquil,
As if he's dreaming
The mesmerised love of strangers

Who inhabit the red tent
Of his ribs, the radiant
Open house of his heart.

Skunk

Night brims with his bittersweet.
Sometimes a squashed body does it: for miles
The highway blows his grief among the trees.

Other times it's fear that burns that incense
In the dark. Or it could be just delight:
Two of them finding one another
Slow and curious
Among moist ferns and cool bluegreen shadows.
Black and white, warm as saliva,
Infinitely, as such things go, desirable.

Making no secret of what's between them,
They hang their lavish presence on the night,
Scattering anarchy in pungent waves
Through the dark beyond your bedroom window.

Night Driving in the Desert

Move fluent as water
Splashing brightness. Imagine
Jackal, badger, wild goat,
Fox-eyes glinting like broken glass:
Gingerly they sniff the sour exhaust.

Remember greenness; name
Its distant children: *ryegrass,*
Olive, avocado, fig—
A first sweetness welling the mouth.

Herbs the Arabs call *ashab*
Sprout inside a single rain,
Rush to blossom fruit seed,
Staining the sand with rainbows.

Imagine a procession of tanager dresses
Drifting through plaited shadow:
Women crossing the earth like water,
Sunlight splashing their skin to stars.

I know it is over in a flash—and after
My heart is beating wildly, wildly for days.

Raeburn's Skater

I want his delicate balance, his
Sturdy, sane, domesticated grace.

Arms crossed, he holds himself together,
Equilibrist of spirit, solid nerve.

Crowblack and solemn, he lives at a tilt
Between limegreen ice and coral air.

Beyond his ken, out of the picture,
The fixed stars hold him fast.

For the Record

After six unsparing days of storm
A grey still day without rain.
Nothing spectacular, no exploding
Stars off the lake, no precious
Glitter of soaked grass, no triumph
In bannering branches, just branches
Taking the air as if it belonged
To them, the faint sleepy *chink-chink*
Of the robin in the next field,
And everything back in its place.
But nothing carnival or sabbatical,
Only a steady domestic peace
Secures all animations in the garden,
Giving everything its due. No fuss,
No unexpected flares, no amazing
Grace in the play and swift trans-
Figurings of light off water. Only
Cloud, seamless still air, this hush.
So, after six days of storm, record
A perfectly ordinary day at last—
Dry, a little on the cool side.

Incident

(for Louis Asekoff)

Mid-October, Massachusetts. We drive
through the livid innards of a beast—dragon
or salamander, whose home is fire. The hills
a witch's quilt of goldrust, flushed cinnamon,
wine fever, hectic lemon. After dark,
while water ruffles, salted, in a big pot, we four
gather towards the woodfire, exchanging
lazy sentences, waiting dinner. Sunk
in the supermarket cardboard box
the four lobsters tip and coolly stroke each other
with rockblue baton legs and tentative
antennae, their breath a wet clicking, the undulant
slow shift of their plated bodies
like the doped drift of patients
in the padded ward. Eyes like squished berries
out on stalks. It's the end of the line
for them, yet faintly in that close-companioned air
they smell the sea, a shadow-haunted hole to hide in
till all this blows over.

When it's time,

we turn the music up
to nerve us to it, then take them one by one
and drop in the salty roil and scald, then
clamp the big lid back. Grasping its shapely fantail,
I plunge mine in headfirst and feel
before I can detach myself the flat slap
of a jackknifed back, glimpse for an instant
before I put the lid on it
the rigid backward bow-bend of the whole body
as the brain explodes and lidless eyes
sear white. We two are bound in silence
till the pot-lid planks back and music
floods again, like a tide. Minutes later,

the four of us bend to brittle pink
intricate shells, drawing white sweet flesh
with our fingers, sewing our shroud-talk
tight about us. Later, near moonless midnight,
when I scrape the leaf-bright broken remains
into the garbage can outside, that last
knowing spasm eels up my arm again
and off, like a flash, across the rueful stars.

Soul Music: The Derry Air

A strong drink, hundred-year-old
schnapps, to be sipped at, invading
the secret places that lie in wait and
lonely between bone and muscle,
or counting (Morse code for insomniacs)
the seconds round the heart
when it stutters to itself. Or to be
taken in at the eyes in small doses,
phrase by somatic phrase, a line
of laundry after dawn, air clean as
vodka, snow all over, the laundry
lightly shaking itself
from frigid sleep. Shirts, flowered sheets,
pyjamas, empty trousers, empty socks—
all risen as at a last day's dawn
to pure body, light as air. Whiteness
whiter than snow, blueness bluer than
new day brightening the sky-lid
behind trees stripped of their illusions
to a webbed geometry
subtler than speech. A fierce blue eye
farther off than God, witnessing
house-boxes huddled together
for comfort, that blindly front
the deserted streets down which in time
come farting lorries full of soldiers.
You are a fugitive *I,* a singing
nerve; you flit from garden to garden
in your fit of silence, bits of you
flaking off in steam and sizzling
like hot fat in snow. Listen
to the pickers and stealers, the shots,
man-shouts, women wailing, the cry of kids
who clutch stuffed dolls or teddy bears

and shiver, gripping tight as a kite
whatever hand is offered. Here
is the light glinting on top-boots, on
the barrel of an M-16 that grins, holding
its hidden breath, beyond argument. And here
is a small room where robust winter sunlight
rummages much of the day when the day
is cloudless, making some ordinary potted plants
flower to your surprise again
and again: pink, anemic red, wax-white
their resurrection petals. Like hearts
drawn by children, like oiled arrowheads,
their unquestioning green leaves seem
alive with expectation.

Totem

All Souls' over, the roast seeds eaten,
I set on a back-porch post our sculpted pumpkin
under the weather, warm still for November.
Night and day it gapes in at us
through the kitchen window, going soft
in the head. Sleepwalker-slow, a black rash of ants
harrows this hollow globe, munching
the pale peach flesh, sucking its
seasoned last juices dry. In a week,
when the ants and humming flies are done,
only a hard remorseless light
drills and tenants it
through and through. Within,
it turns mould-black in patches, stays
days like this while the weather takes it
in its shifty arms: wide eye-spaces shine,
the disapproving mouth holds firm.
                                                  Another week,
a sad leap forward: sunk to one side
so an eye-socket's almost blocked, it becomes
a monster of its former self. Human,
it would have rotted beyond unhappiness and horror
to some unspeakable subject state—-its nose
no more than a vertical hole, the thin
bridge of amber between nose and mouth
in ruins. The other socket opens
wider than ever: disbelief.
                                        It's all downhill
from here: knuckles of sun, peremptory
steady fingers of frost, strain all day and night—
cracking the rind, kneading the knotted fibers
free. The crown with its top-knot mockery of stalk
caves in; the skull buckles; the whole head
drips tallowy tears: the end

is in sight. In a day or two it topples on itself
like ruined thatch, pus-white drool spidering
from the corner of the mouth, worming its way
down the body-post: all dignity to the winds,
it bows its bogeyman face of dread
to the inevitable.

And now, November almost out,
it is in the bright unseasonable sunshine
a simmer of pulp, a slow bake, amber shell speckled
chalk-grey with lichen. Light strikes and strikes
its burst surfaces; it sags, stays at the end
of its brief tether: helmet of dark circles; death caul.
Here is the last umbilical gasp, everybody's
nightmare parent, the pitiless system
rubbing our noses in it. But pity poor lantern-head
with his lights out, glob by greasy glob
going back where he came from: as each
seed-shaped drop falls free, it catches and clutches
for one split second the light. When the pumpkin
lapses to our common ground at last—
where a swaddle of snow will fold it
in no time from sight—I try to take in
the empty space it's left
on top of the wooden post: it is that empty space.

Pieces of Kate

Eleven

Her whole body flowing
into her beginner's
melodies and scales.

Her breakfast talk
all teachers, boys, French
verbs, what her friends

are wearing: electric green
eye-liner, purple tights
spangled with sequins.

Panic and shadows: her dreams
all end in her mother's voice,
a swan at lift-off, some sort

of illumination. She laughs
these frost-bitten mornings
at how her breath smokes

in the car's cold air. When she
leaves and her friends are watching,
her kiss barely brushes

my cheek, though alone
in the kitchen she'll suddenly
hug me hard, or giggle, shivering,

at the way I nibble
the dip in her freckled neck
on the edge of sleep.

Twelve

She visits week-ends. Frayed
by the strain of the distance between us
her voice stays wary.

Curled cat-like on the quilt
her twelve wise years stare past me
to the window, where light

thickens to a violet wash: the world
melting before our eyes. Quickly she
kisses me goodnight, then buries herself

in *The Never Ending Story.* At the far
side of the closed door I listen
to her music-box, its dancer

circling and circling, the tinny tune
slowing, faltering, falling silent
in the middle of a phrase. Last year,

each school-day after breakfast
I'd help her into her winter jacket:
heads bent in wondering silence

we'd walk across the hard white
grass to the car, through a sudden
clamorous, out-of-the-bushes, bursting up of birds.

Thirteen

Her Junior High School graduation:
she's singing alone
in front of the lot of us—

her voice soprano,
surprising, almost
a woman's. The *Our Father*

in French, the new language
making her strange, out there,
full-fledged and

ready for anything. Sitting
together—her mother, her
father—we can hear

the racket of traffic
shake the main streets
of Jersey City as she sings

deliver us from evil,
and I wonder can she see me
in the dark here, years

from belief, on the edge
of tears. Doesn't matter. She
doesn't miss a beat, stays

in time, in tune—while into
our common silence I whisper,
Sing, love, sing your heart out!

A Closer Look

(for Peter Fallon)

Simply that I'm sick of our wars
and the way we live, wasting everything we touch
with our hands, lips, tongues, crowding
the earth with early graves, blind
to the bright little nipples of rain
that simmer on willow twigs, amber shoots
of the stumped willow itself a burning bush
on the scalloped hem of the ice-pond.
So I'm turning to winter beasts instead, their
delicate razor's-edge economies as they
shift for themselves between dens, migrant
homebodies like the souls we used to have,
leaving behind them in the shallow snow
their signatures, the thing itself, illiterate
signs that say no more than *We were here,*
and mean it: handprints, footprints, midnight-
mahogany blossoms of shit, citrus and
mustardgreen swirls of piss that brighten
the eye-numbing, one blank world. Porcupine,
possum, raccoon, skunk, fox—behold them
combing the cold land for a bite, not just
taking for granted their world as it comes
and goes. Wearing weather like a shawl,
they follow their noses through a sphere of
sudden death and instant satisfactions; they lie
in the sunlit pit of sleep, or the worm of hunger
winds his luminous tail to rouse
and send them coldly forth, sniffing the wind
the way lovers browse word by word
first letters for what stays salted
and aromatic between the lines. It isn't
innocence I find in them, but a fathoming
depth of attention anchored in the heart, in its

whorl of blood and muscle beating round—
the way they traffic between frosted starlight
and the gleamy orbs of berries and last apples,
between storm in the big cloud-bearing boughs
and the narrow breath of earthworm and beetle
barely stirring the dead leaves—now all
quivering dash, nerves purring, now the wildfire
flash of pain that lays them, an open secret,
low. I try to make my hopeless own of this,
to sense in myself their calm unthreading
between brisk teeth or busy mycelian fingers,
breaking—as we will—down to our
common ground, the whole story starting over
in the old language: air first, then ooze,
then the solid lie of things, then fire,
a further twist, begin again. Making do.

Staying in Bed

We lay all morning talking. The window
brightens, November-grey to knife-edge blue where
Sunday becomes itself, all bells, without us. The air
flickers, blinks, riddled with starling shadows
or the brusque impulsive blobs of sparrows
flung by hunger. This one touch of winter
makes us face a few home truths: we have to enter
the cold zone naked. Sleepwalker steady, our slow

voices cross the little space between us:
companionable, our bodies stretch; our sex
idles, half asleep, a summer stream
flooding with fernlight green as
early wheat. Such peace: we could be dreaming
away each other's past, digesting hard facts.

Porridge

While you're cooking breakfast
I follow the thread of its smell
back to that first kitchen, where
porridge bubbled on the aster-
blue petals of gas. Bland and
mealy as flour sacks, the smell
used snake upstairs to where
I find myself, half dressed, shivering
before the electric fire's redgold stems
that buzz in blueberry tiles and glow
like the statue of the sacred Heart.

Coffeedark was my father's
morning scent, cigarette smoke
and the acrid black of toast
scorching under the grill. The sharp
rasp of his knife scraped burnt bits
off, butter on: a smell of charcoal
mixed with honeyed gold. Tea
was what the rest of us drank: no smell
unless I dipped my head, felt
steam wreathing cold cheeks, my nose
opening with the word *Ceylon*—
delicate as the bone china
tea-set with apple-green leaf
we used only on Sunday
or for visitors. Sniffing into the cup
like that, I'd picture my mother
bowed above the smoky basin
of Friar's Balsam, madonnaed
by a blue bath-towel, her breathing
a rich mix of phlegm and prayers
for a speedy recovery; the bedroom

a dispensary stew of wintergreen, camphor,
menthol, blackcurrant, Vick's.

If I was up first, I'd cat-pad downstairs
in stocking feet, ease the halldoor open
to bring in the milk I'd heard the milkman
clunk on the porch, empties clinking
at his finger-ends. It was beginning
to brighten: the milk shone white as milk
in its slender bottles, and the *clop clop*
of the milkman's horse, loose harness
jingling, passed up Clareville Road.
Morning smelled frost, a cut-crystal scent
that said another world existed—
clean-cold, intricate as a frozen snowflake,
somehow parallel to ours—hazardous
and dazzling and moonlit-fixed forever.
Sometimes a fresh olivebrown horseturd
smoked on the empty street
like a burnt offering, its racy breath
a summer-pungent mix of oats and meadowgrass
inflaming our tame suburban air. Frost
stiffened filaments in my nose, crinkled
leftover roses, salted the grass, glinted
off the grey pavement. Kitchen smells
seeping from the house behind me,
I'd hug the four cold bottles to my chest,
heel the hall door shut, and hurry
to pour on my porridge the creamy
top of the milk—rich, delicious,
forbidden—before my mother or my father
saw me: smells of sugar, cream, and porridge
marry, and I take that wonder in

like nothing special, till here and now
I hear you tell me from our kitchen
that breakfast's ready, and I rise
to join you, my head swimming.

Men Roofing

(for Seamus Heaney)

Bright burnished day, they are laying fresh roof down
on Chicago Hall. Tight cylinders of tarred felt-paper
lean against one another on the cracked black shingles
that shroud those undulant ridges. Two squat drums
of tar-mix catch the light: a fat canister of gas
gleams between a heap of old tyres and a paunchy
plastic sack, beer-bottle green. A TV dish-antenna
stands propped to one side, a harvest moon, cocked
to passing satellites and steadfast stars. Gutters
overflow with starlings, lit wings and whistling throats
going like crazy. A plume of blue smoke feathers up
out of a pitch-black cauldron, making the air fragrant
and medicinal, as my childhood's was, with tar. Overhead
against the gentian sky a sudden first flock whirls
of amber leaves and saffron, quick as breath, fine
as origami birds. Watching from a window opposite,
I see a man in a string vest glance up at these
exalted leaves, kneel to roll a roll of tar-felt flat; another
tilts a drum of tar-mix till a slow bolt of black silk
oozes, spreads. One points a silver hose and conjures
from its nozzle a fretted trembling orange lick
of fire. The fourth one dips to the wrist in the green sack
and scatters two brimming fistfuls of granite grit:
broadcast, the bright grain dazzles on black. They pause,
straighten, study one another—a segment done. I can see
the way the red-bearded one in the string vest grins and
slowly whets his two stained palms along his jeans; I see
the one who cast the grit walk to the roof-edge, look over,
then, with a little lilt of the head, spit contemplatively
down. What a sight between earth and air they are, drenched
in sweat and sunlight, relaxed masters for a moment
of all our elements. Here is my image, given, of the world
at peace: men roofing, taking pains to keep the weather

out, simmering in ripe Indian-summer light, winter
on their deadline minds. Briefly they stand balanced
between our common ground and nobody's sky, then move
again to their appointed tasks and stations—as if they were
amazing strangers, come to visit for a brief spell
our familiar shifty climate of blown leaves, birdspin. Odorous,
their column of lazuli smoke loops up from the dark
heart of their mystery; and they ply, they intercede.

At Home in Winter

1.

We sit across from one another
in front of the fire, the big logs
clicking and hissing. Outside
is bitter chill: locust branches
grow brittle as crystal. You
are sewing a skirt, your pursed mouth
full of pins, head singing with
Greek and Latin. You frown
so not to swallow any pins
when you try to smile at me
slumped under the *TLS* and bewailing
the seepage of my days, the way
my life runs off like water, yet
inexplicably happy at this moment
balanced between us like a tongue of flame
skiving a pine log and seeming
to breathe, its whole involuntary life
spent giving comfort. It would
be a way to live: nothing
going to waste; such fullness
taking off—warm space,
a fragrance. Now the sight of you
bending to baste the blue skirt
before you pleat and sew the waistband in
enters and opens inside me, so
for a second or two I am an empty center,
nothing at all,
then back to this home truth
unchanged: you patiently taking
one thing at a time as I can't
and all the while your head beating
with hexameters and foreign habits. I go on

reading in silence, as if I hadn't
been startled into another life
for a fiery instant, inhaling the faintly
resined air that circulates
like blood between our two bodies.

2.

Blown in from the noonwhite bite of snow
I find the whole house fragrant as a haycock
with the soup you've stirred up, its spirit
seeping into closets, curtains, bedrooms—
a prosperous mix of chicken stock, carrots,
garlic, onion, thyme. All morning
you've wreathed your head in it, and now
you turn to me like a minor deity of earth
and plenty, hands dipped to the wrist
in the flesh of vegetables, your fingers
trailing threads from the mound of bones
glistening on the counter-top. You stand
at the edge of a still life—glazed
twists of onion skin, papery garlic sacs,
bright carrot stumps, grass-green delicate
stems of parsley, that little midden
of bones—and I behold
how in the middle of my daily life
a sober snow-bound house
can turn to spirit of chicken, air
a vegetable soul, and breathe on me. Turning
back to the stove, wooden spoon
still steaming, you say
in no time now we'll sit and eat.

Four Deer

Four deer lift up their lovely heads to me
in the dusk of the golf course I plod across
towards home. They're browsing the wet grass
the snow has left and, statued, stare at me
in deep silence, and I see whatever light there is
gather to glossy pools in their eight mild,
barely curious but wary eyes. When one at a time
they bend again to feed, I can hear the crisp
moist crunch of the surviving grass
between their teeth, imagine the slow lick of a tongue
over whickering lips. They've come from the unlit
winter corners of their fright to find
a fresh season, this early gift, and stand
almost easy at the edge of white snow islands and
lap the grey-green sweet depleted grass. About them
hangs an air of such domestic sense, the comfortable
hush of folk at home with one another, a familiar
something I sense in spite of the great gulf of strangeness
we must look over at each other. Tails flicker
white in thickening dusk, and I feel their relief at
the touch of cold snow underfoot while their faces
nuzzle grass, as if, like birds, they had crossed
unspeakable vacant wastes with nothing but hunger
shaping their brains, driving them from leaf to
dry leaf, sour strips of bark, under a thunder of guns
and into the cold comfort of early dark. I've seen
their straight despairing lines cloven in snowfields
under storm, an Indian file of famished natives, poor
unprayed-for wanderers through blinding chill, seasoned
castaways in search of home ports, which they've found
at last, here on winter's verge between our houses and
their trees. All of a sudden, I've come too close. Moving
as one mind they spring in silent waves
over the grass, then crack snow with sharp hard

snaps, lightfooting it into the sanctuary of a pine grove
where they stand looking back at me, a deer-shaped
family of shadows against the darker arch of trees and
this rusting dusk. When silence settles over us again
and they bow down to browse, the sound of grass being
lipped, bitten, meets me across the space between us. Close
enough for comfort, they see we keep, instinctively,
our distance, sharing this air
where a few last shards of daylight still
glitter in little meltpools or spread a skin
of brightness on the ice, the ice
stiffening towards midnight
under the clean magnesium burn of a first star.

Wing Road

Amazing—
how the young man who empties our dustbin
ascends the truck as it moves
away from him, rises up like an angel
in china-blue check shirt and lilac
woolen cap, dirty work-gloves, rowanberry
red bandanna flapping at his throat. He plants
one foot above the mudguard, locks
his left hand to a steel bar
stemming from the dumper's loud mouth,
and is borne away, light as a cat, right leg
dangling, the dazzled air snatching at that black-
bearded face. He breaks to a smile, leans wide
and takes the morning to his puffed chest—
right arm stretched far out,
a checkered china-blue wing
gliding between blurred earth
and heaven, a messenger under the locust trees
that stand in silent panic at his passage. But
his mission is not among the trees:
he has flanked both sunlit rims of Wing Road
with empty dustbins, each lying on its side,
its battered lid fallen beside it, each
letting noonlight scour its emptiness
to shining. Carried off in a sudden cloud
of diesel smoke, in a woeful crying out
of brakes and gears, a roaring of monstrous
mechanical appetite, he has left this unlikely radiance
straggled behind him, where the crows—
covening in branches—will flash and haggle.

Morning: The Twenty-Second of March

All the green things in the house
on fire with greenness. The trees
in the garden take their naked ease
like *Demoiselles d'Avignon.* We came awake
to the spider-plant's crisp shadow
printing the pillowcase
between us. Limp fingers of steam
curl auspiciously from the cup
of tea I've brought you, and a blue-jay
screeches blue murder beyond the door.
In a painting over the bed
five tea-coloured cows stand
hock-deep in water at the broad
bend of a stream—small smoothback stones
turtling its near margin. A brace
of leafy branches leans over it
from the far bank, where the sun
spreads an open field like butter
while all the cows bend down
to the dumbfound smudge of their own faces
in the flat, metallic water. And here
this minute, at the bristle tip
of the Scotch pine, a cardinal
starts singing: seven compound metal notes
equal in beat, then silence, then
again the identical seven. Between
the sighs the cars and pick-ups make,
relenting for the curve with a little
gasp of gears, we hear over the road
among the faintly flesh pink
limbs and glow of the apple orchard
a solitary dove throating three sweet
mournful *Om,* then falling silent, then—
our life together hesitating in this gap

of silence, slipping from us and becoming
nothing we know in the swirl
that has no past, no future, nothing
but the pure pulse-shroud of light, the dread
here-now—reporting thrice again
its own silence. The cup of tea
still steams between your hands
like some warm offering or other
to the nameless radiant vacancy at the window,
this stillness in which we go on happening.

FROM *As If It Matters* 1992

That Ocean

To love the scrubbed exactitudes
and the dimmer thing
that shivers at the brink.

There is, for example, the intimate rustle
of this woman's loose skirt, rayon,
as she hurries up a flight of stone steps
ahead of me: I slow down to relish
the faintly kissing sound of threads,
threads and flesh.

Or under a quilted bundling-up of cloud,
a crow's broad black wing
palping air: dark assemblage
of force and voice, appetite and air—
a poise, a bouyancy, a beating
of bone light as breath, burning with purpose.

I despair of dealing sincerely
with the crow, the brushings of desire,
that woman's headlong motion, the black farewell,
steady caresses opening the air,
inflamed soliloquy of the skirt,
fragrant dialogue of flesh and texture.

Under this abrasive rain
the grass, dead all winter,
glows like straw-spun fabled gold,
and two kinds of willow
—the local and the Babylonian—
flush and swell demented: one rises
in upright ecstasy, the other
overarched with grief. Between them
they occupy the air

with embering green and bleached amber
in which, when the rain grows less,
I can hear the little singers
going mad again.

Or there is the absolute intimacy
of eating. To stand in the kitchen
sniffing a bowl of duck fat
is to catch a scent the creature never had
of itself: it is offering up
its essence, the way
neck feathers offered once
an iridescence to the eye one morning,
swivelling in front of you
on a flat dazzle of water. And so
our own essence
is by nature beyond us
and will be rendered after.

At uncommon intervals of attention
we remember ourselves
at one with the world: we enter
the network, a thicket of stillness
where in early spring a sapling of apple or cherry
sends out where it stands
inside the wire fence containing the graveyard
spray after spray of blossom
to stagger the eye
at the solid grey threshold
of gravestones scoured by rain. And this

may be, you imagine, what
in the dream of good government
Lorenzetti's Peace is dreaming

where she lounges
relaxed, empty, ready for anything—
for the end of art, is it,
or simply listening
to what might happen, the clasp
of dancers in a ring, their linked hands
a finished circle? Through it all, all
this seething, I walk
beneath a black umbrella,
behind a bright bead-curtain of rain.

Breaking Points

(for Joe Butwin)

They'll all break at some point,
if you can only find it, he says, hoisting
the wedgeheaded heavy axe and coming down with it
in one swift glittering arc: a single *chunnk,*
then the gleam of two half moons of maple
rolling over in the driveway. He finds
his proper rhythm, my strong friend from the west,
standing each half straight up,
then levelling swinging striking
dead centre: two quarters fall
apart from one another
and lie, off-white flesh shining,
on the cracked tarmac. I stand back
and watch him bend and bring to the chopping-place
a solid sawn-off wheel of the maple bough
the unexpected early snow brought down
in a clamorous rush of stricken leafage, a great weight
he walks gingerly under
and gently settles. When he tests it with his eye

I remember a builder of drystone walls
saying the same thing about rocks and big stones,
turning one over and over, hunting its line
of least resistance, then offering it a little
dull tap with his mallet: the stone, as if he'd
slipped the knot holding it together, opened
—cloned—and showed its bright unpolished
inner life to the world. Joe goes on logging
for a furious hour, laying around him
the split quarters, littering the tar-black driveway
with their matte vanilla glitter. Seeing him
lean on the axe-shaft

for a minute's head-bent silence
in the thick of his handiwork,

I remember standing silent at the centre
of the living-room I was leaving for the last time
after ten years of marriage, the polished pine floor
scattered with the bits and pieces
I was in the aftermath taking with me,
the last battle still singing
in my head, the crossed limbs of the children
sofa-sprawled in sleep. And as soon
as he finishes and comes in, steam
sprouting from his red wet neck
and matted hair, dark maps of sweat
staining his navy blue T-shirt, I want to say
as he drains his second glass of lemonade

that this is the way it is
in the world we make and break
for ourselves: first the long green growing, then
the storm, the heavy axe, those shining remnants
that'll season for a year
before the fire gets them; that this is the way
we flail to freedom of a sort,
and—after the heat and blistering deed of it—
how the heart beats in its birdcage of bone
and you're alone
with your own staggered body, its toll
taken, on the nervous verge
of exaltation. But I say nothing, just pour
more lemonade, open a beer, listen
to the tale he tells

of breakage back home—the rending-place
we reach when the labouring heart
fails us and we say
What now? What else? What?
                                        And now
in the dusk assembling outside the window
I can see the big gouged maple
radiant where the bough stormed off,
and the split logs
scattered and bright over the driveway—in what
from this Babylonian distance looks like
a pattern of solid purposes or the end of joy.

Circlings

The little electric hum of her nerves
under my hand; her lungs
humming our latest air. The garden
a bed of dead leaves
where a young bird is born again
out of the cat's soft jaws. Milkblue,
the two eyes shine in her head.

—

Singing her hundred words for milk
she takes our noiseworld in. But what
in the marvelling moment's
span of her attention
can she make of the frost feathers
glinting in the bedroom window,
or the single fish-eye of light, olive-yellow,
swimming in oil in the slim bottle
after her bath? My face
floats down—a spiked cloud
of flesh and freckles, a sphere
of hairy thunder. My hand
is a sea anemone
in a pool of air, my crook'd finger
a shy beast brushing something
she can feel she feels.

—

In the corner, under a nightlight,
you sit in the rocking-chair
feeding the baby. From my pillow
I see the shadow-shapes
the two of you knit together:
how the line of your neck and throat
vanishes into the sweep of your hair

shawling the small bald crown of her head
that's pressed against
one full breast. Your hands
catch light, moulding the globe of shadow
her head composes, steadying
that wool-bundled body
to your flesh. Wherever I look
in that world of light and shade,
the two of you are touching
each other, leaving me
feeling exiled, not unhappy.
And she's asleep, and I'm asleep,
when you stretch your
warm length again beside me.

—

When the sun glares in the window
and I leave our bed, the baby
is lying beside you,
a half smile on the lips
round your nipple: her eyes
are closed, your eyes
are closed, your head lightly resting
on top of hers. Downstairs,
geraniums and pink impatiens
press their flushed winter faces
to the dining-room window,
and everywhere circles
are slowly spinning
in circles, shadows dancing
through rings and widening rings
of light.

Cows

They lay great heads on the green bank
and gently nudge the barbed wire aside
to get at the sweet untrodden grass, ears
at an angle flicking and swivelling. Something
Roman in the curled brow, massive
bony scaffolding of the forehead,
the patient, wary look that's
concentrated but detached, as if
the limits of being didn't matter
behind such a lumbering surge of things
in the flesh. Yet in their eyes some deep
unspeakable secret grudge—in part, perhaps,
their perfect knowledge
of the weight of the world
we hold them to. And something Dutch
about that recumbent mass, their couchant
hefty press of rumination, the solid globe
folded round the ribs' curved hull, barrelling
that enormous belly. The close
rich cud-smell where they stood
grinding down grass to milk
to mother us all; or the childhood stink
of stalls—all milk and piss and dungy straw:
what that umbered word, *cowshed,* conjures.

I remember an Indian file of cows in mist
moving along the lake's lapped margin,
a black and white frieze against the green hill
that leaned over them: the sound
of their cloven steps in shallow water
reached me like the beat of a settled music
in the world we share, and they could have been
plodding towards Lascaux, or across
broad prairie-seas of green, even

trampling water-edges such as this one—
trudging through our kingdom-come
of sagas and cattle-raids. Heads bent,
they stepped into mist and silence, the pooling
splash of their hooves a steady progress
that seemed to go on forever, forged
for an eternal trek to grass.

I love the way a torn tuft
of grassblades, stringy buttercups and succulent clover
sway-dangles towards a cow's mouth, the mild teeth
taking it in—purple flowers, green stems and yellow petals
lingering on those hinged lips
foamed with spittle. And the slow chewing sound
as transformation starts: the pulping roughness
of it, its calm deliberate solicitude,
entranced herbivorous pacific grace,
the carpet-sweeping sound of breath
huffing out of pink nostrils. Their eyelashes
—black, brown, beige, or white as chalk—
have a miniscule precision, and in the pathos
of their diminutive necessity
are the most oddly human thing
about them: involuntary, they open, close,
dealing as our own do
with what inhabits, encumbering,
the seething waves and quick invisible wilderness
of air, showing the one world
we breathe in
and the common ground—unsteady
under the big whimsical hum of weather—
we all walk across
one step at a time, and stand on.

Sea Dog

The sea has scrubbed him clean
as a deal table.
Picked over, plucked hairless,
drawn tight as a drum—
an envelope of tallow
jutting with rib cage, hips, assorted bones.
The once precise pads of his feet
are buttons of bleached wood
in a ring of stubble. The skull—
bonnetted, gap-toothed, tapering
trimly to a caul of wrinkles—
wears an air
faintly human, almost ancestral.

Now the tide falls back
in whispers, leaving the two of us
alone a moment together. Trying
to take in what I see, I see
the lye-bright parchment skin
scabbed black by a rack of flies
that rise up, a humming chorus,
at my approach, settle again
when I stop to stare. These
must be the finishing touch, I think,
till I see round the naked neckbone
a tightly knotted
twist of rope, a frayed noose
that hung him up or held him under
till the snapping and jerking stopped.
Such a neat knot: someone
knelt safely down to do it,
pushing those soft ears back
with familiar fingers. The drag end

now a seaweed tangle around legs
stretched against their last leash.

And nothing more
to this sad sack
of bones, these poor enduring remains
in their own body bag. Nothing more.
Death's head here
holds its own peace
beyond the racket-world of feel and fragrance
where the live dog bent, throbbing
with habit, and the quick children
now shriek by on sand—staring,
averting. I go in over my head

in stillness, and see
behind the body and the barefoot children
how on the bent horizon to the west
a sudden flowering shaft of sunlight
picks out four pale haycocks
saddled in sackcloth
and makes of them a flared quartet
of gospel horses—rearing up,
heading for us.

Two Climbing

1.

After the blackface sheep, almond coats daubed
to the blush of slaughtered innards,
all I saw going up was a small frog
speckled rust and raw olive, slick
as a lizard, with a lizard's fixed
unblinking eye. It splays and tumbles
to a safe shadow
where heather-roots wind through limestone
while I keep climbing
behind Conor, who's twelve, my heart
starting to knock at thin air, effort. He loves
leading me on, and when I look up
to where he stands waiting—legs apart and
firmly planted on a rock spur, gazing round him
at the mountains and the sea, the thin
ribboning road beige below us, my figure
bent over the flat green hands of bracken—
I'm struck sharp as a heart pain
by the way this minute brims
with the whole story: such touched fullness
and, plain as day, the emptiness at last.

2.

Once down again, safe home, we both
look wondering up to the top of Tully Mountain
and the barely visible concrete plinth
that peaks it, on which he sat
exalted for a time and took
the whole of Ireland in, he said,
with one big swivelling glance, and took

twelve snaps to prove it: a windy shimmer
of cloud, mountain, water—a rack
of amphibian spirits drifting
over our heads. I saw the way our elevation
simplified the lower world
to rocky crops and patches, neat
green and tea-brown trapezoids
of grass and bog, bright pewtered spheres
of pure reflection. We sat out of the wind
on two flat rocks, and passed
in silence to one another
another sweet dry biscuit
and a naggin whiskey bottle
of water, pleased with ourselves
at some dumb male thing for which
he finds the word: *adventure.* Going down,
he lopes, leads, is deliberately solicitous—
pointing out loose rocks, the treacherous
bright green surface of a swampy passage,
a safer way. Non-stop, his knowing talk
enlarges airily our trek and conquest.

3.

Walking at last the field path to the house,
he is all straight spine and limber stride
in his mudded wellingtons,
while I note how stone silent
the plum-coloured broad back of the mountain is,
keeping the wind off our lives
in this hollow. Before going in,
he sets on an outside windowsill
the horned sheep skull we've salvaged

from the bracken, weathered to a cracked adze
of jawbone ringed and bristling
with broken teeth. Bone-flanged, the great
eye sockets gape, and like fine stitching
the skull's one partition
seams dead centre.
In less than a week from now
he'll have forgotten this bony trophy,
but not the journey we took together
to find it: that hammering brisk ascent, the luminous
view of everything, those buffeting winds, the one
unruffled interlude of quiet, then, in the end,
that sweet leading down. While I'll go on
seeing the split skull—colour of crushed almond
or washed-out barley muslin—shine.

What Remains

Limegreen silken wings of two luna moths
pulsing gently on the shadowed screen door
all morning. A stretch of thigh
bared in sunlight: silksmooth and tanned between
sandalwood and dry sherry. A faint
scarlet fleck along one cheekbone, white
twist of silk scarfing the throat. Mooncurve
of a brick-pink fingernail; tonguetip
vanishing behind a gleam of teeth
or travelling—all fleshed texture and blood-heat—
the nicked lip, making it glisten. A black smudge
thickening a single eyelash, and under a light
rose-checkered dress the long outline
of a leg, a solid shadow. One hand splayed
on the breathing rise and fall of a brown belly:
white starfish on a rock; a stencilled palm
come to light on a cave wall
where torches reel and leap
across the dark. Or else
it is a calf-length skirt of early mist,
a blouse birchleaf green, one goldspiked
lavender glitter of garnets, a sandal's
spiralling leather strap, jangling brass anklets,
or the sudden juddering ripple of a hip
as the breath stops and then
comes back again in time. Such
abandoned bits and pieces
as my seagull eyes pick over—
that quicken in me, rising
to mind as whole bodies,
and all their covered, incandescent bones.

Kitchen Vision

Here in the kitchen
where we're making breakfast
I find my own view of things
come to light at last: I loom, huge
freckled hands, in the electric kettle's
aluminum belly. In there

the lime-green fridge, military files
of spice jars, and that transfigured window
where the sun breaks flagrant in,
must all recede, draw off, and join
the tiny mourning face
of Botticelli's Venus
hung above a Lilliputian door. In there

all our household effects
are strictly diminished, pared down
to brilliant miniatures
of themselves—the daily
ineluctable clutter of our lives
contained, clarified, fixed in place
and luminous in ordinary light
as if seen once and for all
by Jan Steen or Vermeer. And off

in the silver distance the baby
stares at me from her high chair
of a minute's silence,
and you—a mile away at the stove
turning the eggs—turn round
to see me gazing
at my own sharply seen
misshapen self in the kettle
that's just starting to sing,
its hot breath steaming.

The Cave Painters

Holding only a handful of rushlight
they pressed deeper into the dark, at a crouch
until the great rock chamber
flowered around them and they stood
in an enormous womb
of flickering light and darklight, a place
to make a start. Raised hands cast flapping shadows
over the sleeker shapes of radiance.

They've left the world of weather and panic
behind them and gone on in, drawing the dark
in their wake, pushing as one pulse
to the core of stone. The pigments mixed in big shells
are crushed ore, petals and pollens, berries
and the binding juices oozed
out of chosen barks. The beasts

begin to take shape from hands and feather-tufts
(soaked in ochre, manganese, madder, mallow white)
stroking the live rock, letting slopes and contours
mould those forms from chance, coaxing
rigid dips and folds and bulges
to lend themselves to necks, bellies, swelling haunches,
a forehead or a twist of horn, tails and manes
curling to a crazy gallop.

Intent and human, they attach
the mineral, vegetable, animal
realms to themselves, inscribing
the one unbroken line
everything depends on, from that
impenetrable centre
to the outer intangibles of light and air, even
the speed of the horse, the bison's fear, the arc

of gentleness this big-bellied cow
arches over her spindling calf,
or the lancing dance of death
that bristles out of the buck's
struck flank. On this one line they leave
a beak-headed human figure of sticks
and one small, chalky, human hand.

We'll never know if they worked in silence
like people praying—the way our monks
illuminated their own dark ages
in cross-hatched rocky cloisters
where they contrived a binding
labyrinth of lit affinities
to spell out in nature's lace and fable
their mindful, blinding sixth sense
of a god of shadows—or whether (like birds
tracing their great bloodlines over the globe)
they kept a constant gossip up
of praise, encouragement, complaint.

It doesn't matter: we know
they went with guttering rushlight
into the dark; came to terms
with the given world; must have had,
as their hands moved steadily
by spiderlight, one desire
we'd recognise: they would—before going on
beyond this border zone, this nowhere
that is now here—leave something
upright and bright behind them in the dark.

Woman at Lit Window

Perhaps if she stood for an hour like that
and I could stand to stand in the dark
just looking, I might get it right, every
fine line in place: the veins of the hand
reaching up to the blind-cord, etch
of the neck in profile, the white
and violet shell of the ear
in its whorl of light, that neatly
circled strain against a black
cotton sweater. For a few seconds

she is staring through me
where I stand wondering what I'll do
if she starts on that stage of light
taking her clothes off. But she only
frowns out at nothing or herself
in the glass, and I think I could
if I stood for an hour like this
get some of the real details down. But
already, even as she lowers the blind,
she's turning away, leaving a blank

ivory square of brightness
to float alone in the dark, the faint
grey outline of the house
around it. Newly risen, a half moon
casts my shadow on the path
glazed with grainy radiance
as I make my slow way back
to my own place
among the trees, a host of fireflies
in fragrant silence and native ease
pricking the dark around me
with their pulse, ungovernable, of light.

Compass Reading

This morning, the cat pawed up
against the glass storm-door, her eyes
wild and satisfied, a quiver
of pale grey-brown feathers
between her jaws. Shouting,
slamming open the door, I rescued
the broken neck, closed eyes, the tuft
and ruffled wings—the breast
still soft and warm—and placed them
out of harm's way, as if it mattered,
in the mailbox. Later,
under cover of the dark,

I took and threw the titmouse
among the leaves still clinging to trees and hedges
at the back of the house: flying
from my hand it gave, I thought,
the smallest sigh, the way
it broke the air, the air
opening for it, taking its little weight
for the last time, before it fell
with a faint, desiccated splash
among twigs and leaves
where it will lie, grow less itself, unravel
back to bone, to mould, to dust,
to next year's fierce leaf
whose feathers and fine airs
will stand up to anything. I imagine
its first arrested screech, the cat
tasting a salt smear of blood
across tongue and teeth: she knows
the ripe smell of death, the face
of terror, the terminal spasm.

These days I seem as heartless as a lock
that is all innards and bitter tongue:
wherever my ears go, they hear
nothing but clocks ticking, each tick
a distinct penetration of air, a pulsebeat
greeting its own goodbye. I can see
in the shortlived gauze of dew on the steps
the neat dark footpads of the cat,
who will—for all her satisfactions—
not be appeased.

Station

We are saying goodbye
on the platform. In silence
the huge train waits, crowding the station
with aftermath and longing
and all we've never said
to one another. He shoulders
his black dufflebag and shifts
from foot to foot, restless
to be off, his eyes wandering
over tinted windows where he'll sit
staring out at the Hudson's platinum dazzle.

I want to tell him he's entering into the light
of the world, but it feels like a long tunnel
as he leaves one home, one parent
for another, and we both
know in our bones it won't ever
be the same again. What is the air at—
heaping between us, then
thinning to nothing? Or those slategrey birds
who croon to themselves in an iron angle
and then take flight—inscribing
huge loops of effortless grace
between this station of shade and the shining water?

When our cheeks rest glancing against each other,
I can feel mine scratchy with beard and stubble, his
not quite smooth as a girl's, harder, a faint fuzz
starting—those silken beginnings I can see
when the light is right, his next life
in bright first touches. What ails our hearts? Mine
aching in vain for the words
to make sense of our life together; his
fluttering in dread

of my finding the words, feathered syllables
fidgeting in his throat.

In a sudden rush of bodies
and announcements out of the air, he says
he's got to be going. One quick touch
and he's gone. In a minute
the train—ghostly faces behind smoked glass—
groans away on wheels and shackles, a slow glide
I walk beside, waving
at what I can see no longer. Later,
on his own in the city, he'll enter the underground
and cross the river, going home
to his mother's house. And I imagine
that pale face of his
carried along in the dark glass, shining
through the shadows that fill the window
and fall away again
before we're even able to name them.

Breakfast Room

1.

The words have always stirred a sudden
surge of light, an air of new beginnings, something
neat and simple, a space
both elemental and domestic—because, perhaps,
they bear a sort of innocent sheen
of privilege, a room so set apart
for an event so ordinary, a glimmer of ritual
where mostly we know only broken facts, bits and pieces
stumbling numbly into one another. Here
is a murmur of voices, discretion's homely music
of spoons on saucers, the decent movements
people make around each other—eager
to let themselves become themselves again
after the uncertain journeys of the night. Or it may be
the secret knowing smiles that lovers save, sitting
to face each other in their quaint conspiracy
of hope and saying, *Pass the milk, please,* but meaning
Nothing has ever pleased me more
than how your naked shoulders and the small of your back
lay on my spread hands; your earlobe, tongue, wide eyes
entering half-frightened mine in the dark.

2.

And in Bonnard's *The Breakfast Room,* you'll see
the impeccable ordinary order he finds in things:
white, slateblue, the tablecloth bears its own still life
of teapot, cream pitcher, sugarbowl,
china cup and scalloped saucer, the half glass of raspberry juice,
bread in yellow napkins, that heaped dish
of purple figs and a peach. And, as if

accidental by the French windows—
through which morning light
passes its binding declarative sentence
on every detail—a woman stands
almost out of the picture, her back
against the patterned drapes, dressed to go out
and giving a last look back, her eyes and strict lips
asking directly, *You think this*
changes anything? Yet she too
is part of this stillness, this sense
that things are about to achieve
illumination. Beyond the window
a stone balustrade, and beyond that
nature's bluegreen tangle tangles
with the light that's melting one thing
into another—blue, scrubbed green, strawgold,
a house with a white and lilac roof
at the end of a sunstreaked avenue
on which the summer trees are
blobs of turquoise. Inside, quite distinct,
that woman is held to her last look back,
her sudden pulsebeat shaking
all the orderly arrangements
of the table. Through its
ambivalence of light, its double tongue
of detail and the world at large,
we are brought into the picture, into a kingdom
we might find under our noses: morning's
nourishment and necessary peace; a pause
on the brink of something always
edging into shape, about to happen.

Two Gathering

After supper, the sun sinking fast, Kate and I
have come to the shore at Derryinver
to gather mussels. Across cropped grass, rocks,
we walk to the water's edge where low tide
has exposed a cobbling of cobalt blue shells, others
tucked in clusters under a slick fringe
of seaweed. In my wellingtons
I enter shallow water, bending over
and wresting from their native perch
the muddy clumps of molluscs, rinsing them
in salt water that clouds and quickly clears again
as the tide laps, a slow cat, against me, then
pushing my handfuls into the white plastic bag
I've laid out of the water's way on seaweed.
Kate, in sneakers, is gathering hers
off dry rocks behind me: almost sixteen,
her slim form blossoms in jeans
and a black T-shirt, long hair falling over
as she bends, tugs, straightens
with brimming hands, leans like a dancer
to her white bag, looks out to me and calls
So many! Have you ever seen so many! her voice
a sudden surprise in that wide silence
we stand in, rejoicing—as she always does
and now I must—at the breathless plenitude
of the world, this wondrous abundance
offering itself up to us as if we were
masters of the garden, parts of the plenary
sphere and circle, our bodies belonging
to the earth, the air, the water, fellow creatures
to the secret creatures we gather
and will tomorrow kill for our dinner.

When I bend again—my hands pale groping starfish
under water—it's Kate's own life I fumble for,
from the crickets singing her name
that September afternoon she was born
to the balance she strikes
between separated parents, her passion
for maths, the names of her lost boys,
or the way she takes my arm
when we take a walk on Wing Road
or up the hill from Tully to the cottage. This instant
I can feel her eyes on my bent back, seeing me
standing over my ankles in water, the slow tide
climbing my boots, my cautious
inelastic stepping between elements
when I place the mussels I've gathered
in the bag. And if I turn to look, I'll see
a young woman rising out of sea-rocks, bearing
the salmon and silver air on her shoulders,
her two hands spilling a darkblue arc, about
to take a dancer's step: I hear the muffled clack
of live shells filling her bag.

In our common silence we stay
aware of one another, working together,
until she calls out—*Have you seen*
their colours? Brown and olive and bright green
and black. I thought they were only navy blue—
delighted by variety, the minute ripple of things
under water or changing in air, the quick patterns,
as if the world were one intricate vast equation
and she relished picking it over, seeing the figures
unfold and in a split surprising second
edge out of muddle into elegant sense, the way
she's explained to me her love of maths

as a journey through multiple views to a moment
of—she said it—*vision,* you simply see it
all in place before your eyes: a flowering branch
of impeccable sense, number and grace
shimmering in a single figure, a shard of truth
shining like the head of a new nail
you've just, with one stroke, driven home.

Feeling the drag and push of water, I know it's time
to move and I do, inching backwards, my hands
still scrabbling under rubbery weed-fronds
for the mussels' oval stony bulk, their brief
umbilical resistance as I twist them
from their rock, swirl in water, add them
with drippling chill hands to the bag, sensing
the summer dusk falling all over us. *Dad look! A heron!*
standing not twenty yards from us
on the hem of the tide: a grey stillness
staring at nothing
then flicking his serpent-neck and beak
into the water and out, taking a single deliberate step
and then on slow opening wings
rising and flap-gliding across the inlet, inland, heavy
and graceful on the air, his legs
like bright afterthoughts dangling. *He's so big,*
she calls, *How does he do it?* and across
the raw distance of rock and water I call back,
It's the span of his wings, he uses the air,
thinking about question and answer, the ways
we're *responsible* to one another,
how we use our airy words to lift us up
above the dragging elements we live in
towards an understanding eloquent and silent
as blood is or the allergies I've handed

to her system—our bodies' common repugnance
to penicillin, sulfa—all the buried codes
that bind us in a knot even time
cannot untangle, diminishing, in a way,
the distance between us. *Did you see,* I hear my voice,
his legs? The way they dangled? Thin—
her voice comes back to me—*as sticks,*
and the colour of pearl. Funny
how he tucked them in, putting them away,
and she drops a castanet handful
of mussels into her bag.
My hands
are blueish, a small breeze riffles water,
the spur of land we're on
is drowned in shade: we've gathered enough
and it's time to go. She watches me wading
through bright, light-saving pools, reaches
a helping hand when I clamber up rock
above the seaweed line where she stands waiting
on grass the sheep have bitten to a scut,
their tidy shit-piles of black pellets
scattered all over. With pleasure we behold
the two bulging bags I've draped
in glistering layers of olivebrown bladderwrack,
both of us thinking of the dinner we'll have
tomorrow: brown bread, white wine, a green
salad, the steaming heaps of open shellfish
—ribboned in onion, carbuncled
with chunks of garlic—the plump dull-orange
crescent of each one gleaming
in its mottled shell, sea-fragrance curling off
the greybright salty peppered soup
they've offered up to us, and in it the brilliance
of lemon wedges swimming. At least once each summer

we have a family feast like this, and I picture
her delight in dipping buttered bread, laying
a hot mussel on her tongue, the squirt of sea-tang and flesh
against her teeth, sipping the wine that's
still a stranger to her palate, remembering
the way the sun went down behind the two of us
as we gathered dinner, as if our lives
were always together and this simple.

Now

we stand side by side for a minute or two
in silence, taking the small bay in and the great shade
spreading over sea and land: across the water,
on a sloping headland of green fields, we see
how a stopped hand of sunlight still
in the middle distance lingers, brightening
one brief patch of ground with uncanny light
so I cannot tell if I'm looking at a moment past
of perfect knowledge, or a bright future
throbbing with promise. Then Kate
is giving me, again, her words: *I wonder*
will it strike us over here, is what
I hear her say—her words, unanswered,
hanging between us as we turn to go.

FROM *So It Goes* **1995**

Pause

The weird containing stillness of the neighbourhood
just before the schoolbus brings the neighbourhood kids
home in the middle of the cold afternoon: a moment
of pure waiting, anticipation, before the outbreak
of anything, when everything seems just, seems *justified,*
just hanging in the wings, about to happen,
and in your mind you see
the flashing lights flare amber to scarlet
and your youngest daughter
in her blue jacket and white-fringed sapphire hat
step gingerly down and out into our world again
and hurry through silence and snow-grass
as the bus door sighs shut
and her own front door flies opens and she finds you
behind it, father-in-waiting, the stillness in bits
and the common world restored as you bend
to touch her, take her hat and coat from the floor
where she's dropped them, hear the live voice of her
filling every crack. In the pause
before all this happens, you know something
about the shape of the life you've chosen to live
between the silence of almost infinite possibility
and that explosion of things as they are—those vast
unanswerable intrusions of love and disaster,
or just the casual scatter
of your child's winter clothes on the hall floor.

Outing

Granted the Atlantic between us, I can only imagine
walking in on you asleep in an armchair
the nurses have pillowed, your white-haired head
and the powdery skin of your face tilted sideways,
your chin sinking into the sag of your breast
where one button in the pale blue frock's undone.

When you fell down that Sunday last summer
and your poor shoulder buckled under you,
I could tell—trying to lift that terrible weight
from the lavatory's slippery stone floor—
the way things were. Still, as every other summer,
you loved our drives out of Bloomfield
to the sea, loved sitting in the car up Vico Road,
staring off over water towards Howth or Bray,
Greystones, the Sugarloaf (as plain on a good day,
you'd say, as your hand). And no matter
even if it rained, it was always a cleansing
breath of fresh air for you, a sort of tranquil
hovering above things, the known world
close enough to touch: blackberry bushes
and high-gabled houses; foxglove and bracken;
the hundred steep steps down to the sea.
I used to wonder if it ever crossed your mind
that the next life you firmly believed in
might be something like that—the same peace
of simply sitting, looking at whatever was there
and passing: older couples with their dogs,
salted children streeling from the sea,
a parish priest swinging his black umbrella,
the occasional brace of lovers in step. Over
the lowered window you'd smile
your genteel "Good afternoon!" to them all,

and seem for this little while at least
almost out of reach of your old age—its slumped
and buzzing vacancies, blank panic, garbled talk.

But now, near another summer, they tell me
your temperature flares, falls, flares again,
and nothing to be done. Alive, they say,
but in ways not there at all, you've left us
and gone on somewhere, and I remember
how as kids we trailed your solid figure
when you pushed the youngest in his pram
and turned to call us all to catch up, *Hold on*
to the pram now, don't let go. I remember
the pounding silence when you'd hide
and all of a sudden come dashing out
behind your voice—your arms like wings,
laughing our names to the air around us,
the sound of your glad breath bearing down.
But when I appear in a week or so, I'm told
you won't know me, the way you mostly
don't know the others, and I remember
your phrase when I'd come home at last
after months at school: *I wouldn't know you,*
you'd say, holding me away at arm's length
or in a hug, *I just wouldn't know you,*
only this time the same delighted words
will die in your mouth, and you'll be
two puzzled milk-pale hazel eyes
staring at this bearded stranger. You've left
already, knowing well what I've no words for:
the smudge and shaken blur of things, bodies
floating by like clouds, brittle sunshine
flapping through a window to your lap,

days in their nameless, muffled procession,
or the frank night-scurry of dream after dream,
each with its seepage, bat-flash, dear faces.

Here among the woods and hills of New Hampshire
it's you I think of when I watch the mountains
appear and disappear in mist, the shape of things
changing by the minute. Were you with me now,
I'd show you these blowsy irises, and those
exploding globes of rhododendron, lady slippers
in the shade, or flagrant and shortlived the blaze
of the yellow day-lilies. You could listen out
for the pure soul music the hermit thrush makes
alone in the echo-chamber of the trees, his song
a blessing, you'd say, to your one good ear.
Side by side, we'd sit in this screened gazebo
facing Mount Monadnock, and you might try
the mountain's name a few times on your tongue,
getting it wrong, wrong again, until
you'd give your helpless laugh, give up, and say
For God's sake don't annoy me, will you,
whatever you call it. Can't I just call it
Killiney, Sugarloaf, or Howth—what matter?
We'd agree on this, *God knows,* and you
would sit back to enjoy the view, the delicious
sense of yourself just sitting—the way
we've always done, we're used to—pleased
for the moment with what we've got,
and pleased at how that big green hill
swims in and out of view as the mist
lifts and settles, and lifts, and settles.

Night Figure

She hovers over the ache of thresholds: that brass
doorknob and the cream paint chipped at the jamb
enter her face again, so close she doesn't notice.

She needs to hear us breathing, the three of us
pitching into sleep in the one room, tucked in
by a faint smell of face powder, sticky touch of lips.

Snare-beat of rain on the roof, the rain spitting
against the window. *It's spilling rain,*
she'll say to herself, *he'll be drowned out in it.*

As if underwater, she stands listening
to the house and all its stunned tongues
gather round her heart. Rumours of being

rush into the instant: a bus coughs by
on Clareville Road, quick footsteps
syncopate through rain, a bicycle bell

jings in the dark; *squeek squeek* of pedals
against wind and hill. When she moves
into their front bedroom, she sees

from the window a hurrying figure, hears
the little brickish *klik* that high heels
make on stone. A deep pain starts

to open in her heart, and she's the secret
goings-on in hives—a slow gathering
and transformation, the finished, overflowing

golden comb. Nothing now, *nothing*—
till his key comes fumbling the hall-door,
then the sudden rush of air

as the door shuffles open, raw
against the hall's linoleum. Hint of stagger
in the hallway; heavy sit in the muffled chair—

his lidded eyes haze over, blinking: two hearts
heaving like mad. Behind closed doors
the air listens to a huffle of voices. She can feel,

when the petals of pain and rage
have closed again, her vacant relief: the house
complete at last: she can sleep. So

she lies beside his breath, her eyes open
and our house a hive of silence
round her head, her splitting head. Fingernails of rain

tapping for help against the window: *Let us in,*
let us in, can't you? Then thickened stillness
levels the dark, taking the bed

she lies on, and she slides—nothing stops her—
into the wooden dusk
of wardrobes, down the sheer drop of sleep.

Headlines

I knock on the tree. It opens
into my mother's grave: a beech tree
coming into leaf. Wan green
springlight: one wind-up wren
clicking for cover, making her bed
in a tenement of dead wood.

The border crawls
along these little hills the ice
let fall: it could almost be invisible
but for just what happens:
one more bedroom mirror in bits
and shivers, the spreading chill.

'Victims,' they say, 'killers'—
running out of words. The ice
waits for a change of heart. Here
is a girl's head, a man's hand
holding the gun against it: she feels
the small round point of it for a second.

Ordinary days. Spring's slow
explosions all over the place:
beech leaves, maybush, lacy
sprays of laurel, cherry blossom's
pink boudoir. Such a crush
of shameless life, you'd forget everything

except this jeepful of soldiers
patrolling the estate, buttoned-up
and clutching sten-guns. In her last years
my mother never read

beyond the headlines: *It isn't real,*
she'd say, folding the paper
and going back to her window,
How could it be?

Angel Looking Away

Somewhere they are throwing
rice and rosewater,
carrying the coffins shoulder-high.

But on Pisano's pulpit the angel
is turned away in sorrow
from the slaughter of the innocents

and in the interrogation center
a man has turned
away from the polished steel table

on which a man—
calloused tallow soles
stretched towards us—is twitching

as a live wire
wide as its own glitter
kisses the eye of his penis

while another man
is gazing down, perplexed,
at the naked figure on the table,

and holding a small black box
with two switches: between
a thumb and tapered index finger

one switch is being gently eased
to the ON position, and now
the poem is looking

at the angel looking away,
at that handsome strong youth
in his marble sorrow,

and you know
it can do nothing,
not to lose its tongue.

Swan in Winter

There is this enormous white sleep.
No marks visible on the soft body
sprawled on saltgrass in a few inches
of rocking water, the long neck
limp as water and flopping back
when you lift and let go, hauling it
out to the solid ground of shells
and seawrack, twilight lights winking
at the wide mouth of the Sound.

Orange beak, black legs and feet
blatant in that mass of white:
the lovely whole creature could be
asleep on the empty shore
in a settled silence dense with questions.
But you've nothing to say to this solid
apparition dropped from a seal-grey sky
swollen with snow, the cold
biting through wool and goosedown,
the swan still warm when you
bury your bare hands in whiteness.

That such a great heart could stop
without a sign, those mighty wings
fold over one another for the last time
like that, the live body come to be
just a letting go in the cold, as easy
as entering at first the water, then
take hold of it taking hold and ride
the known currents, companionable
in the friendly element: imagine
those eyes closing, a deeper dark
than their own coming down, this
Paschal candle of a bird snuffed out.

There is this solid feel of bone
inside the wing you've opened,
a hinged brightness wide as
a whitewashed wall, all the life
seeped out of it, your own hinge-
winged hand the stronger, this huge case
hollow, heavy, immense, bereft,
but ruling in its white absence
the whole foreshore. It is its own
quartz grave, glittering as Newgrange,
and through it the old swan stories
come floating back, wings singing.

You twist with difficulty
one wingfeather out, pulling
until it comes reluctantly
to hand, lamenting the indignity
but wanting that unfading white
to keep catching light
on your windowsill, contain
this riddling death, this
inexplicable huge conclusion
from (is it?) natural causes.
The quill weighs almost nothing
in your hand, the air in its shaft
electric, each ferny perfect barb
a lit shiver in the breeze.

Chill nips your naked hand
while this deep sleep suffers
no change, although every second
you expect a shuddering roll, the
sleeping beauty to stretch itself
under your touch, the knobbed head

jerk upright, those closed eyes
to open staring into yours
for a moment of pure knowing
as both of you say the one word, *Death,*
to one another, and it will wrench
its white tent of breath and blood
away, its force flooding back, the way

we want resurrections over
and over—of your father fallen back
on his hospital bed, his mouth
gaping after its last breath; your mother
cold in her padded coffin, cheeks
chill as glass, hard as bone;
or your friend sitting crosslegged
on the kitchen floor, a crooked
bloodstring hung from his nose,
hands held open in his lap as if
giving everything away; and you
waiting for their eyes to open
just once more, to say that
all's been known, all understood
at last, all taken in the one embrace
that is the whole body's grace and
affirmation in spite of all, as now

here, again, hoping against hope
the bird will wrench its bones away
and lean up, neck rising like some
great stalk, the head a blossom,
and flatfoot it cumbersome back
to water, wings flowering
into full sail, and floating on the cold
until it feels fit to change elements

again, and will thrust, run, rise—
to ride the sudden loving surge
of air, and rising, *Oh!* off and away
into the surprised twilight like a white flame.

But of course it doesn't move
a muscle and you close home
its fanned-out wing and leave it there,
wondering what will happen next—
a high tide take it back, or gulls,
or the rats who inhabit holes in the rocks,
or crows strutting their live black
ravenous appetites all over
this white field.
Leaving as always
without answers, you see the inlet
lit up by three swans taking off
like gunshot, heraldic wings
hoarding all the light that's left
in the late day, letting you hear
the musical breath of their beating
as they pass over your head and
swerve inland, as you turn yourself
inland again, past the roofers' hammers
banging echoes up the wooded hill,
and past the redbellied woodpecker
glimpsed for an instant as it enters,
vanishing, a dead yellow locust.

Whistling in the Dark

1.

The day of her waking and last exposure, I saw
the dark cloud of a tree against the light
and thought of the various ways a body had
of being invisible: all that stolid wood and breathing leaf
washed out to an airy presence
in the dismembering energies of light. Later,
unprepared, I would see the breathless, full,
provisional rigidity of death, that loved body—lit
by its history—become a lump of wooden absence
wearing a flowered nightie and the ghost of a smile.
Just another way of being invisible: the temple
stunned; cheeks fleshy but cold as stone; locked hands—
and nothing to break the silence between us
but the sound of my escaping breath as it brushed
over the open secret of her *not-here, not-here.*

2.

At dusk near water I watch the waves, the luminous rain,
and a plover scurry over rocks and weed,
whistling to its hunger. Through gathering mist
the foghorn moans, and the hiss of rain on my head
turns me towards town again, which is all of a sudden
lit up and glittering, as if there were some pattern to it
after all. The bird prods a small rock, and I hear
the splash and wriggle of something alive under there
and a whistle of excited hunger. Silence. Then the blind cry
of warning off water. The world gets smaller and smaller. Time
to go home, and I start—swallowing those two big words as I go.

3.

When I stand with my right hand touching the back
of her crossed hands, I can tell without looking
that the livid veins and that bright traveller, the blood,
have settled for snow at last. Aflame once
in the friendly element of air, heartsfire beating in tongues,
they've fallen asleep in a snowbank, breathing a small hole
in the cold, and sliding in—as a snake in winter
makes a space to sleep and wake in. So, pulling the air
in their wake, these ardent pilgrims have turned
to a world of snow, leaving nothing but a little melt-mark
behind them, shape of a starched white nightdress—
where tiny red flowers have all this while been blooming.

4.

Out early this morning, I see ebony pellets of deer shit
glinting with dew, and on moss filaments a few first
fractures of light. The white of a broken mushroom flashes
like a fish turning at the surface, or could be the gleam
of a piece of steamed plaice laid open before her eyes
delighting in it, the fork dipped then wavering to her mouth,
all lost for one unfrightened instant
in the shriven intimacy of expectation, taste, the moister instincts
ticking over. And I have, across the table, nothing to say—
trying to fix this minute among its poor relations.

Horses

1.

Although they seldom muscled above me,
I remember being dwarfed always
in the stone fountain of their force,
rawly afraid, awe-struck at something
vast, a violence harnessed and hauling
a cart of scrap metal through our tidy suburb,
men with wild, weatherbeaten faces
snapping the reins. The neck's
thick branching grace I remember,
and the fleshed bones in their legs
that I saw from the footpath or, once,
watching a blacksmith bend to them
in a forge in Terenure, and lift one
and fold it neatly over in his aproned lap
and touch the crescent foot
with a big file or pliers: the instrument
a glimmer in his blunt hand, the whole
horse-bulk rippling into shadow.
A few times, too, I felt tender rough lips
touch my hand that held, flat-handed,
a snatch of grass, fearing the teeth
but staying still until—grass gone
in a quick crunch—I had my hand back
to pat the silky nose, finger-comb
the mane, slap sleek hindquarters
and the belly big as a currach, to feel
the heat simmering there, the nervous
flickering along skin as if the veins
were charged, the blood itself electric,
and knowing how heavy the flesh was
from the way my hand lay on it
like nothing, a straw on water. I'd imagine

it all falling on me, or being lost
under a flail of hooves, the feel
of so much live involuntary flesh
capsized over my own bones
in a fury of bared gums, a trampling
froth-storm white at the mouth,
two black moon-mad eyes on fire.

2.

Remote, perfect, overwhelming
how they inhabit space
by crowding out the air they occupy;
and yet contained, confined inside
some glorious force field of their own:
a solidified smell of oats, sweat, leather,
contemplation, astonishment. The span
and ponder of them absolute
in anchorage, taut as propellors, steady
in that massive confidence of rump
and hindquarters, thews bulging, everything
sinewy, roped, rounded as sea-shells,
the grand parallellogram of the head
giving millstone definition
to the word *Skull.*

3.

Two white horses in a field up the road:
a mare and her colt gleaming
out of the clouded day, at grass
in a windless wide silence,

the tenderness between them palpable
as that mild and serious something
in an empty chapel. The young one
is lying down, while his mother
browses a close circle round him,
but when she stops to stare at
the sound my footsteps make
on the road beyond the hedge
at the edge of her world,
the little one rises too and stands
looking, his two coal-black eyes
lingering on my strange shape, letting
out of his lustrous ebony muzzle
a faint, plaintive, interrogative
whickering.

I know they're abroad
in every weather—wind snapping
at all corners of the valley, rain-squalls
making ditches roar, sunshine
cooking the air in clover—and it is for them
only weather, to be taken
with the same dense patience
they proffer to whatever happens, although
at intervals under a heavy shower,
after they've been standing as still
as creatures carved in quartz,
the mare will suddenly toss and gallop
round the fuchsia-bush and barbed-wire
border of their field, her colt
quickly following, his new legs
slow and a little stiff at first, but then,
with a springy, kicking bound
and a careless, elegant animation
of everything that makes the body

and the body move, he'll cut
to a perfect dash, tuck tight
to a tandem gallop, doubling his mother
on the run—picking up as he goes
whatever he knows from her,
but first how to warm the blood
she's given him, and then
how to be, increasingly, in the world.

Heirloom

Among some small objects
I've taken from my mother's house
is this heavy, hand-size, cut-glass saltcellar:
its facets find her at the diningroom table
reaching for the salt or passing it to my father
at the far end, his back to the window.

The table's a time-bomb: father hidden
behind the newspaper, mother filling
our plates with food; how they couldn't meet
each other's eyes. When he'd leave the table
early for an armchair, *Just a glance at the evening paper,*
she'd sit until—all small talk exhausted—

we kids would clear the tea-things away,
stack dirty dishes by the scullery sink,
and store the saltcellar in the press
where it would absorb small tears of air
till the next time we'd need its
necessary, bitter addition. Now it figures

on our kitchen table in Poughkeepsie,
is carried to the diningroom for meals—
its cheap cut glass outlasting flesh and blood
as heirlooms do. I take its salt
to the tip of my tongue, testing its savour
and spill by chance

a tiny white hieroglyph of grains
which I pinch
in my mother's superstitious fingers
and quick-scatter over my left shoulder,
keepıng at bay and safe
the darker shades.

Ghosts

1.

One by one, in a fringe of frayed light,
they'll enter the narrow room
where you lie in the dark—a stone pressed
between chest and throat, the sting
of salt on your tongue—letting the fragments
reassemble. You'll learn to live
with the curtains drawn, the stammering
smallest breath of them remembered,
and everything you didn't understand
staring back at you
as pure fact, their closed faces.

2.

Sackcloth, the clouds come down as ash.
The scorched word, *Angel,*
drifts up the chimney. Nothing breathes
where the rose window
has lost its magic, dancers wither
into smoke, forlorn gums keep their teeth
agape in a glass of cold water.
And nothing in the dark
but a tuft of beige hair and a wisp of white
whispering at the window, *We have come*
this far. The air
raw as a peeled turnip, a vague
turnip-coloured dawn
daubing the east, the shell of one bell
bringing the snifflers out
to eight o'clock Mass. From the front window

of this widowed house, a face—
though you know it isn't there—stares.

3.

I can see the two of them now
moving slowly over the sand away from me,
grown very small in the growing distance:
her pale blue cardigan; his olivegreen
tweed jacket; the slow roll of her hips;
his straight back. The light hovers, then,

till I see no sign before me, only know
they've entered into a last glimpse
of her hand reaching out for help
over a rocky place, and he stopping
at last and reaching his hand back
for her hand as I hoped he would
before the sun went in and I have to hurry
from a coming shower. They have

become the barest glimmer, as if passed
through a glass wall in air, walking
on the other side of light. For minutes
I see nothing but rocks, the tide
that rises to cover them, taupe-green and
navy-blue tongues foaming closer. Then,

Is that them again? Two tiny figures
float along the far wall of the pier
and are gone, nothing but a shaft of light
clinging a minute to the stone

until it too seems to shiver and enter itself
and go, a luminous late withering, leaving

me to stare at where it was. You take
what you can, even light on stone:
those two hands knowing their own
instant's touch, the exact exchange of that
before the loaded cloud comes over,
slows down light, and shakes it out as rain.

On Fire

How hungrily the wood grown light with weathering
burns, taking its own life till there's nothing left
but blackened fragments on a bed of ash, although it was
all sudden tongues and crackling at the sheer joy
of making its own unmaking like that, this perfumed, rash
expenditure of itself in a reckless cause. I remember
my granny's ramrod back in her widow's weeds,
on her knees in the hearth, bellows in hand, getting
redness to spurt among black coals. Or my mother
laying on their paper bed the sticks of kindling
I'd hatcheted from an orange-box that morning,
arranging the clinker remains of the last fire
and the gleaming nuggets of coal together, then quick
to the kitchen sink, stretching stained hands
away from her apron. Or my father stacking turf-sods
in the dark mouth of the cottage grate: he'd get
the pale blaze going, then stand back to stare
and say, *There now,* with satisfaction, pour himself
a glass of whiskey, fold open the evening paper,
and sit into the old blue armchair we'd later burn
in the garden. Not discreet but daring, fire has its own
wild fling in the face of gravity, finding its wings and
not looking back, living brilliantly for the moment
it becomes nothing and a handful of ash. The ancients
saw souls in it with the heads of beasts, birds,
and spent their lives handing it on, as we did
at dawn each Easter morning, quenching every flame
in the church and then—starting from the dark porch—
bringing the new fire into our lives till the whole place
was ablaze and singing. Unknown soldiers of the world
have poured their own hearts into fire, while houses
of bricks and mortar, steel and glass, have curled up
in the teeth of it like leaves, and blown away. In love,
we are small gods shaking our sandals out as fire,

and at the end we may put our dead in it and gather up
what it makes of them—a few spoonfuls of speckled ash
and some bright purged bone. Its truest rhyme
is with *desire*—sprinting to touch, to act, all desperate
reflexive verb. And now the two of us here in the dark
have let the fire die slowly down, and it's your body
I want to see with the curtains open and the half-moon
pressed against the window: your long pale body
smouldering on top of the sheet, glowing beside mine
while we warm ourselves again in the heavy world
of matter, catching fire at the fire we make of our lives.

Wet Morning, Clareville Road

Under morning greys of rain the roses
are washed, glowing faces, and in near gardens
the limp washing hangs with no hope
although all the slate roofs down Westfield Road
shine like polished chrome. Up early to make
a little door that opens out, a word passage
into the rain-filled air among the flowers
and the morning traffic—as if the words
themselves could offer light, could make
some sense of the muddle in which the heart
flutters. Dark green the overarching
ascension of trees; walled gardens
where scarlet roses are exploding; yellow
the cylinders of chimney pots; luminous
and edgy the fretwork clouds: how things
fall into place when seen from a window, as if
the given were a pattern with precise meanings
and could console us for the loss
of signs and spires and words like *consecration,*
or could speak at least a little comfort
after sounding brass and after
the manic world where men go on
killing as usual, bringing lovely cities down
to rubble, dust, the town of minarets and bells
become a cry in the snipered street, hunger
a dog that howls all night, and out
among the hills not too far north of here
the neighbour-guns and drums keep beating
and repeating their one word—while here
in our apparent peace there's nothing
but the wet hiss of traffic on glistening road,
the stark green shock of a privet hedge,
that bloodthirsty, nude sunburst of roses.

If I went under the rain to smell the roses,
I would inhale your arms, the warm breath
between your breasts, the whole heady
exhalation of you moving by me on the stairs.
Is it because we can't hold onto something
as evanescent as a smell that—when it
finds us again—it brings the whole body
back into our arms, the steady undoing
of straps and buttons, cotton and silk things
drifting from hot skin, a white shirt
forgetting itself and flying
beyond its own down-to-earth expectations?
Shaken by a slight breeze, lace curtains
let light filter through to the room
I only imagine, where a bowl of roses burns
on a low glass table by the window:
blue mutations agitate air; sea salt
stings the tip of the tongue;
and no ghosts, only ourselves, to stand
in that early play of light and its solutions—
which may contain for the moment
time and all its grazing shades. The room
a flowering branch of details: this
brimming glass, this swimming mirror,
these peaches, this open book, this cracked
black and white Spode bowl, these trials of love.

When that space, with its shades of love
and its impossible colours, fades
to the wet morning outside my window,
I see only the tree in the back garden
bowed down as it is every summer
under a rich crop of bitter little apples.
But my brother makes the garden grow

once more, coaxing its flowers into the sun
like those unhappy patients he'll listen to
all day for their broken stories, crying out with joy
at the first start of the begonia
into pale pink blossom. *I thought it was dead,*
he says without thinking, *and now just look at it!*
He can talk of little else,
learning as he is not to grieve
but go on, and will—when he gets himself
out of bed this morning—fill the house
with his good will, looking forward
to whatever happens, ironing his shirts
to the sound of that soprano he loves
singing *Tosca:* when he thinks it's ready,
he'll test the hot iron as our mother would
with a spittled finger, then sing along as he listens
for the startled hiss that steams away
and, like a quick kiss, vanishes.

Firefly

On my last night in the country, a firefly
gets stuck in the mesh of the window-screen
and hangs there, revealing to me its tiny legs,
head like a miniscule metal bolt, the beige sac
jutting under its curl of a tail, splayed
on the fine wire and at intervals sparking,
the sac flashing lime-green, liquid, electric—
on-off-on, again *on-off-on,* then stop—
as if signalling to me in silence,
the trapped thing singing its own song.

For a while I watched it singing its own song
and then, when it went dark for a long time,
I leaned up close to the wire to become
a huge looming thing in its eyes and blew on it
gently, the way you'd blow a faint spark
to fire again—catching a dead leaf, a dry twig,
growing towards flame—and it started to flush
lime-green again, *on-off-on* again, deliberate
and slow, a brilliance beyond description
which filled my eyes as if responding to
the bare encouragement of breath I'd offered,
this kiss of life in a lighter dispensation,
as if I'd been part of its other world
for a minute, almost an element of air
and speaking some common tongue to it,
a body language rarefied beyond the vast
difference between our two bodies, both of us
simply living in this space and making
our own sense of it and, almost, one another.

It's how they talk what we call love to one another
over great distances, making their separate
presences felt in the dark, claiming whatever

the abrupt compulsions of the blood have brought
home to them, then seeking each other out
through the blind static that clogs up the night,
the mob of small voices and hungry mouths
coming between them, that grid of difficulty
they have to deal with if they want in every sense
to find themselves and decode in their own limbs
the complicated burden of this cold light
they've been, their whole excited lives, carrying.

Of course I don't understand their whole lives carrying
this cold light that might once have been a figure
for the soul, the soul at risk, worn on the sleeve,
its happenstance of chance and circumstance and will,
those habits of negotiation between its own
intermittent radiance and the larger dark; of course
the words I reach to touch it with are clumsy
and impertinent, nothing to the real purpose;
and of course it leads its subtle specific life
beyond such blunderings. But it was the smallest
of all those creatures I've come close to, looked—
however dumbly—into, and was still signalling
that last time I breathed its liquid fire to life,
blew my own breath into its brief body and it fell
from the wire like a firework spending itself
into blackness, one luminous blip of silence
into the surrounding night—the way a firework goes
suddenly silent at its height and drifts back down
in silence, blobs of slow light growing fainter
as they fall into the flattened arms of the dark.

But for those moments it inhabited the dark
wired border zone between us, it seemed
as if it could be looking back at me, making

between my breath and its uncanny light
a kind of contact, almost (I want to think)
communication—short, entirely circumscribed,
and set in true perspective by the static-
riddled big pitch dark, but still something like
the way we might telegraph our selves
in short bright telling phrases to each other—
on-off-on then stop—the whole live busy night
a huge ear harking to the high notes
of our specific music, and to the silence
that contains it as the dark contains the light.

At the Falls

Although the lilacs after all that rain have all
gone rusty, the sun's brought summer back
to warm your hair, and brings these three boys
down to the river where the cotton mill once
turned its big wheel, brings them to the flat
rocks at the falls where the swollen water—
colour of tin and tree bark—dawdles slowly
first in its approach and then plunges over,
its darkness transforming in an instant into
light and air as it twists like bolts of cotton
till it strikes the line of jutting rocks and
fountains down and out in a bristle-arc of
wet light, a flare of flashy water unwinding
to the bottom where it goes on recollecting
the vertigo of its last moment aloft, the odd
exaltation of its fall as it leaped, wondering
would it ever be the same, the same again,
and breaking then into a hundred hands
of light, before feeling itself start to be itself
once more—slowed down, flowing away,
changed and not changed but held again
between sensible banks, and not a thing
of wings and terror till the next descent
narrows its throat and it takes the same rush
through its whole headlong body, ready
to cast itself away again, surrender again
to whatever in its own nature keeps it
moving between such formless / formed
expressions of itself, until it loses all
its vast accumulated life to salt.
                                        In khaki shorts,
the three boys gleam like sea beasts, making
their ungainly earthbound way over rocks
to step behind the water screen and stand there

in that numbing roar, and reach their arms
out through it, stiff limbs hovering as if
disembodied, at odds with the steady state
of water-chaos that stretches back to when
first water began to make its creepy way
in the world, map the whole outlandish route
to its own undoing. The boys just stand there
in the deafening bliss of water—bodies behind,
arms in front, an image of its bottom line:
how it will not stay, how we're behind
and ahead of it at once—their young triumphant
flesh in water, who have not surrendered to, but
know, its near danger, *drunkenness of speed,*
the way it offers endless assent to gravity
by going over, going down, some of it flying off
as mist, pure spirit in the shock of boiling
almost against its nature, while the rest becomes
a heavy froth of light unfolding, struck thunder.

And still

the eye's tugged back from what has happened
to what's about to happen, back to black water
with the luminous stain of tree bark through it
as it dawdles to the falls *(again!)* and then *(again!)*
taking the plunge, the rocks breaking it to brilliant
atoms of itself, another life if only for an instant.
Forgetful of their own flesh and pride of the flesh,
the boys stand still inside the noisy heart of water
and stretch their arms out, aiming crazy laughter
at each other, water striking and splashing
off their arms as if off fountain creatures
you'd stumble on around a cobbled corner
in Rome, and pause at the sight of the sleek
limbs of horses, thighs of gods, those glistening
torsos, nipples, fingers. Above the clamour,

the boys are calling one another, convinced
they've entered and are at home for the moment
in the secret depths of this other element. Still
the water won't stop and you watch it
refuse nothing, plunge and recover itself
from fall to fall, in terrible kinetic love with
gravity and going on, to rise somewhere
in fragrant dusk among jasmine and oleanders,
adrift, infinitely receptive and never-ending
like *the calamity of death,* till it makes a music
you couldn't have intended or imagined, the ceaseless
stream of it brimming, without intervals, the air,
overflowing the ear, pure vigour taking its separate
self-absorbed life away in—always—the other direction.
Now

the sun falls on the water and the arms projected
from the water, which will soon grow tired
of their own daring, this making strange of themselves
and the common element, and the sun falls
on your own head where you stand on the footpath,
warming your hair. As one who sleepwalks,
you sweat uphill again, find your way home
and fall into a deep sleep, your head become
one stanchless wound of sound and movement
streaming away, an opening to what could be
nothing but change, yet stands, a constant thing,
and flesh in the midst of it our signature saying
we belong, saying nothing stays.

Ants

A black one drags the faded remains of a moth
backwards over pebbles, under blades of grass.
Frantic with invention, it is a seething gene
of stubborn order, its code containing no surrender,
only this solitary working frenzy that's got you
on your knees with wonder, peering into the sheer
impedimentary soul in things and into
the gimlet will that dredges the dead moth
to where their dwelling is, the sleepy
queen's fat heart like a jellied engine
throbbing at the heart of it, her infants
simmering towards the light. On your table
a tiny red one picks at a speck of something
and hurries away: one of its ancestors
walked all over the eyes of Antinous, tickled
Isaac's throat, or scuttled across the pulse
of Alcibiades, turning up at the Cross
with a taste for blood. In a blink, one enters
your buried mother's left nostril, brings a message
down to your father's spine and shiny clavicle,
or spins as if dizzy between your lover's
salt breasts, running its quick indifferent body
ragged over the hot tract of her, scrupulous
and obsessive into every pore. And here's one
in your hairbrush, nibbling at filaments
of lost hair, dandruff flakes, the very stuff
of your gradual dismantling. Soap, sugar, a pale
fleck of semen or the blood-drop from a mouse
the cat has carried in, it's all one grist to this mill
that makes from our minute leftovers
a tenacious state of curious arrangements—the males
used up in copulation, females in work, life itself

a blind contract between honeydew and carrion,
the whole tribe surviving in that complex gap
where horror and the neighbourly virtues, as we'd say,
adjust to one another, and without question.

Shed

You wouldn't know it had been there at all, ever,
the small woodshed by the side of the garage
that a falling storm-struck bough demolished
some seasons back, the space and remains now
overcome by weeds, chokecherry, wild rose brambles.
But at the verge of where it stood, a peach tree
I'd never seen a sign of before has pushed
its skinny trunk and sparse-leaved branches up
above that clutter into the thoroughfare of light
and given us, this Fall, a small basketful of
sweet fruit the raccoons love too and sit at midnight
savouring, spitting the stones down where the shed
used to stand, those bony seeds ringing along
the metal ghost of the roof, springing into the dark.

FROM *New Poems* **1993–1995**
IN *Relations: New & Selected Poems* **1998**

Place

First morning back, there's a faint cap of cloud
on the brow of Tully Mountain, flash of a blackbird
between sycamore and ash, glint of dew on a few daisies
the scythe has spared. Lilies of the valley stand

in a battered can, the cover of my mother's prayerbook
wrinkles with light, and my neighbour's rickety mutt
mumbles a crust of stale bread. In early sunshine
the houses across the lake seem solid as chateaus, seem

as if they'd stand forever. High-arched, their barns are
granaries of light, though the old cottages lie like bones
over the open fields. And here, slightly apologetic,
comes the cough of the cock pheasant, stepping

among potato drills as if he owned the place: crimson
and cinnabar his head, his feathers cinnamon and gold,
he will hide in his own life down there
where whins and heather and boggy grass can flourish,

and the sunny morning be sheer heaven to him.

Sunshine, Salvation, Drying Shirt

Between the big window and the lake's blind flashes
I hang my line of Sunday washing, most of it grey
or black, one shirt ecclesiastical white so you'd think
a priest was tucked away here off the beaten track
where—perched on the cross of the ESB pole—a kestrel
fills my head with Hopkins and his windhover
which I caught the other evening standing on air
unbuckled, almost stopped there, so I could spot
when the bird tilted—silhouetting itself—the crucifix
the poet must have seen, a sign bringing Christ
into the picture, causing the creature to buckle and
give off blood and fire, making a holy show of itself.

Flies hum, skiving a shaft of sunshine, and a chaffinch
dabs at the bread I shared with him for breakfast: could I
have been, I wonder, a monk of the Ninth Century,
my heart, too, in hiding, *stirred for a bird,* and finding
God's fingerprints on everything? Drowsing outside,
the book of Bashō fallen from my lap, I hear the note
a chaffinch makes, breaking day in half, then gone, then
another answering with a little run of song, then silence
as the summer air lets go of them, teaching us how.
In his cell, the monk bends to scratch his ankle, watch
an ant at work, or opens the door to take the day to heart,
as, in a word-flurry, Father Hopkins blesses himself
before his bird can terminate its dive and take the life of
something hidden in the grass—a mouse, a lark—stabbing
through the neck and biting its head off. Meantime,

sun's a wonder on the back of my hand, my splayed shirts
keep shadow-boxing on the line, and a million midges dance
like dervish angels on a pinhead of light. When such days
stretch their slow-burning bodies out for us, it's hard to believe
the incredible weather won't hold up, as we want it to,

forever. But it won't, and even in the middle of its comforts
I know the flies gyring my head like atomies of air
would, given half a chance, make a quick meal of these
pulpy eyes. Still, with the last cleansing drop dripped out,
my clothes grow lighter in the light breeze, becoming
crisp as souls new-shriven, and from high in the heavens'
cloudless blue comes a twangy drumming as a snipe
shows off its climbing power—its silvered body all
bat-flap and ascension against the open sky—then turn
and curve, twist and fall, angling its tail-feathers to
make music from its own body falling like that, as if
singing the risk itself for the frightful pleasure of it.

Near Mount Kurokami, Bashō changed apparel and his name,
then stood behind a waterfall and looked straight out
at what kept going. Next daybreak he was *off again*
on unknown paths. Here, pinned to its place, my white shirt
is all puffed up, I see, with its own bright life—a full sail
going nowhere—and in this silence that's come down on us
now towards evening like a cloud of light, the iron sound
of the Angelus bell beats round and round the valley.

In Late February

As when the siege of some great city lifts

and they sit outside on steps drinking hot tea
and making mindless chatter, I hear my daughter
after two months of snow and a sudden thaw
—feeling sun heat the hair at the back of her neck—
say the word *grass* over and over, seeing a strip
of pale green the robins are already mining.

Driving to work last Sunday, I thought the soul
might be a handful of blown snow, its scattered
shattered light vanishing before my eyes.
And yesterday, from a maple branch, I could taste
the barest trace of sweetness, encased
in a blade of ice where the branch had fractured.

Every night now, under the blazing stars
and over the ice cracking like toffee brittle,
a dog barks all night like my mind, keeping
the entire neighbourhood awake. But when
I meet the barefoot boy in the coloured waistcoat
walking home past midnight in a cloud of song

I know the old season is almost over,
and I almost love my own shadow again—
its attached levity making light of obstacles
and accelerating over known ground
like a catbird lost in the deep leaves of summer
but for its persistent, *pursue-me!* music.

Unfinished

The house next door but one to this one
never happened, and all connected with its
shadow life are shadows now and maybe
tremble in the grass-blades growing where
the planked earthen floor would have lain
between two walls facing east and west,
the front to where morning light still spills
over the bony shoulder of Diamond Hill,
the back taking in a flank of Tully Mountain
and the valley where the Atlantic evening
scatters its last handfuls.

A half-built
shell of stone, it seems to stand as if
just broken from a dream, stunned,
its rags and tatters of raw stone
standing as a solitary gable, a single wall,
the big lintel-piece balanced almost on air,
the dead handiman having neatly slotted
stone to different stone like the syntax
of a language that once trusted itself
and the sense it was making, left no gaps
of incoherence, nothing unsaid, knew
exactly how things fitted, could tell
the perfect place for any solid shape
that could be gathered from the field itself
into which it's lapsing now
a few stones at a time, but mostly—in time
as we measure it—standing up to cows,
rough winds, persistent rain.

I'm told
the man who layered its stones left it as is
when the family of the wife he'd intended
denied permission. So he left and went
to America, they say, though no one knows

what happened to the woman. What
could her eyes have done, I wonder,
when she passed this way in the wake
of two cows, or going to Mass on Sunday?
I can't imagine the pause she'd make
on the far side of the sally bank, drenched
fuchsia brushing her shawl, that gaping
half-made body looking blankly back at her,
and beyond it—through what would have been
their bedroom wall—the sheen of the lake
they'd have seen with some wonder
under a hundred lights. Somewhere
in Chicago or South Boston it may be
he tried a while to remember, or couldn't
help the hard walls his hands had put up
falling across his sleep, and then nothing.

I know the house I live in is—under its
whitewashed mortared skin—the same as his,
although it folded round itself, was finished,
and the weather that enters is a play of light
through glass, only the safe sounds of rain
on the roof or wind in the chimney. But
I love what he left, blunt masterpiece as it is
of understatement, its tight-lipped simplicity
getting the point across in its own terms
and caring for nothing but the facts
of the matter, the exact balance between
how this gesture registers in the world and
how the hard thing that happened, happened.

Stop

We slowed and pulled over beside the body
on a side-road in the valleyed shadow
of two blunt hills near Sligo. With its
digger's claws, dust-encrusted pelt, a darkened
curl of blood between bared teeth, the creature
lay as if asleep, flies gilding it, when I stopped
the engine and got out to see my first badger,
a solid black and white case of absence,
and she got out too, took one quick look,
then walked across to the clump of bushes
briaring over a high bank, leaned in
among the brambles, and began picking
the fat blackberries till she had enough
to bring two handfuls and spill them
on the flat dashboard, where they glistened
onyx and veiny vermilion when we
took them one by one and put them
in each other's mouth, splitting
each plump-fleshed bitter-sweetness
between our teeth, tonguing and swallowing
this dark ripeness. We drove on then,
the green after-rain peace of that deep valley
holding us a half-hour more
till we found the main road and turned
north on it into the thundershower
that would wash the badger's blood
away from our stopping-place, but not
the memory of it, nor of love
fenced round by barbs and brambles
yet flourishing among the fruits of the earth
and filling her hands for me.

One Morning

Looking for distinctive stones, I found the dead otter
rotting by the tideline, and carried all day the scent of his savage
valediction. That headlong high sound the oystercatcher makes
came echoing through the rocky cove
where a cormorant was feeding and submarining in the bay
and a heron rose off a boulder where he'd been invisible,
drifted a little, stood again—a hieroglyph,
or just longevity reflecting on itself
between the sky clouding over and the lightly ruffled water.

This was the morning after your dream of dying, of being held
and told it didn't matter. A butterfly went jinking over
the wave-silky stones, and where I turned
to go up the road again, a couple in a blue camper sat
smoking cigarettes over their breakfast coffee (blue
smell of smoke, the thick dark smell of fresh coffee)
and talking in quiet voices, first one then the other answering,
their radio telling the daily news behind them. It was warm.
All seemed at peace. I could feel the sun coming off the water.

Woman with Pearl Necklace

—VERMEER, 1664

Since he painted her, she will always be putting this pearl necklace on
in her own ordinary room of light, the shaded yellow of it washing

to pure white where a wall becomes a painted nothing, a figure
for what he knew but could name no other way: the sheer intensity

of being this young woman this moment this morning, meeting
her own mirrored gaze, its marriage of modesty and rapture, and feeling

Me I am here it is I that is all I can see how they gleam how I seem
as her hands draw the ribbons that hold the band in place, fingers

lightly touching each other, the two hands between them seeming
to measure something—the weight the word 'soul' could bear, maybe,

to her eyes in the glass—the soul itself, it seems, assembled for once
on the very brink and fleshly lid of things, its image not the glass

nor the leaded window through which morning light finds her,
but that wall of all colours making white, which the painter faces.

Six O'Clock

Steamy mushroom weather. Under the white pines
a smell of turpentine and dust. A young woman
swings by, her handbag the colour of ten-year-old claret.

In the cemetery someone is playing a mouth-organ:
There's No Place Like Home rises on the surprised air
while light-leaved saplings nod eager affirmatives

to each other *(yes yes, that's it, exactly!),* stop a minute
to take things in, then again to affirmation.
I can smell the one pine tree cut down this morning

and carted away, leaving only this white stump of a thing
and its glimmer of dust, the lingering scent of resin. Airborne,
a glitter-flock of starlings expands, contracts, expands

like a beating brain, a heart pulsing, its every element
answerable. Our cat sees with her ears, each swivelling
to catch the drift of things on the breeze, as I go on

naming one thing at a time *(orchard, silo, hawk, eyelid,*
sea-mark, bloody cranesbill, slate) making windows
to peer into . . . exactly what? The hour that's in it?

Oasis

To enter this cool space
settles the stutter of nerves
that has taken your gaze
from the tall blue fall

of mountains in the distance:
you step into a ring of shade
in which you find this deep,
reflective, necessary source,

this simple joy
the committed body catches at
as if at the last gasp
of home: first the felt

luxury of shadow, its way
of slowing you down to know
what flesh is again, then
that sound the pool makes

stirring at its banks
and from the heart. *Water. . . .*
you keep saying
its wedded syllables

as if they were enough,
their open and closing vowels
a cry before satisfaction,
though when you reach

its very self—the hard bright
splash of it—it's something
speechless, simply known,
the fluent pure give of it

first to the fever of your skin
and after
to that naive but greedy need
your tongue knows:

it fills, overspills
the heart in your mouth
like another life
gasping all its secrets at once,

and everything grows clear
as day breaking
through muslin curtains
to keep you here, where breath

swims in the saturated radiance
we came from, as if
two could go on saying
at the same time

the one good word.

Fenceposts

Inside each of these old fenceposts
fashioned from weathered boughs and salt-bleached branches
(knotholes, wormy ridges, shreds of bark still visible)
something pulses with a life that lies outside our language:
for all their varicose veins and dried grain lines,
these old-timers know how to stand up
to whatever weather swaggers off the Atlantic
or over the holy nose of Croagh Patrick
to ruffle the supple grasses with no backbone—
which seem endlessly agreeable, like polite, forbearing men
in a bar of rowdies. Driven nails, spancels
of barbed wire, rust collars or iron braces—the fenceposts
tighten their hold on these and hang on, perfecting
their art and craft of saying nothing
while the rain keeps coming down, the chapping wind
whittles them, and a merciless sun
just stares and stares: yearly the land is eaten away
and they'll dangle by a thread until salvaged
and planted again in the open field, which they bring
to an order of sorts, showing us how to be at home
and useful in adversity, and weather it.

FROM *Still Life with Waterfall* 2002

Aubade

Walking Renvyle strand at sun-up, I see a gull
that's in the right place at the right time

turn to a bird of fire. And here on a slope of sand
I see an otter must have had to scramble, his big foot

dragging, his unwavering concentration stapled
to the prey he must be—I want to say—*imagining,*

its flesh and blood a little persistent detonation
in his brain, the salt-blue hugeness of the Atlantic

only a cloak he wears at dusk and dawn. *Thereness*
is all: that burn of chance and quickened breath of appetite

adding up to all that this world offers—
glitter and shadow, pang of absence, the way

this day keeps coming on: we meet; we disappear.

Man Making the Bed

Psalm after psalm into a dead sea of silence, inventing
their own enormous, endangered day. Scalded, lord,
by sunlight and the lizards watching, licking dust,

he unfolds the fresh sheets: brisk sniff of laundry, white
as a field of Queen Anne's lace. The word 'linen'
comes to rest, a cleansing breath, and a big sail bellies

in the breeze he conjures, speaking its memory of flax and water,
acres of raw linen in the Low Countries or the near North
laid out like a waiting canvas, a picture-glimpse of heaven

with a few shriven women's bodies adrift in it, dazzled
by its dear, old-world, breathing spaces. He billows the sheet
and a wondercloud swells in this small room, a huge

snow-ruffle drifting down, a tabernacle of cool white
rising in the desert. Here is the bed new made, and here
its play of flesh and spirit, unsettling themselves in bodies.

He is alone here, making the bed up, stopped
between the solidity of things as they are and the huge white peace
of the sheet-sail flapping from his hands for a matter of seconds

and subsiding, spread flat, its corners pointed
towards where she leans—half-dressed in memory,
one soft stroke of daylight streaking her spine—

to draw taut the sheet he's holding the other side of
and they snap together, lay it flat, tug it tight together
in what looks like a fullness of time and truth

and not plummeting asunder. Lying alone
between the sheets tonight, feeling the clean of them,
their white arms tight about him, he will dream

a wilderness of tents in moonlight: asleep,
they will be shivering a little, as if they felt the stars
press their silverchill rivets in, or the future

with red eyes whispering to rouse them.

Painter's Diary

Notations only. Dog-star weather. Marble tiles. Shutters.
A vase of marigolds glowing in the dusk. Dark outline
of a leg-curve. Flesh-coloured streak of arms. Hedges
lemon-blue. Spheres of gleam where trees were, or a razor's
telling edge of light at the door jamb. One smudged hand
holding a cut pomegranate. On the mirrored tablecloth
he finds the *broken white* of a dress and its bone-coloured
buttons. Half-open doors. Silver twist of olive leaves
after rain. Flesh under water. Eyes behind glass. Thirsty
cloudburst of azure grapes. Soon enough, he thinks,
they're dust. But just look at them—shining now
in the great breath of things and night coming. A gathering
of light and air. A mouth. Dusk-glow. Gold of marigolds.

Fallen Branches

Tree-thickened, the night's a field of fireflies, tiny star-tics
bright as mercury, love-signs in the scented here and now
which the thunder he hears grumbling in the distance
will douse and scatter, drowning leaves and hacking open
the dark with its bombard riverrun body and its white-hot
electric dishevelled wings. Yesterday, he kept finding

fallen bits of branches eaten by weather, by just what is
in earth, in air: breakdown and decay. *Death,* he'll say
from a sanitary distance, but what of the live one
stormed at, brought down and torn asunder in that full
breath and pulsing—so he has to step back, nothing to say,
wishing the slightly fuzzy sticks of cinnamon fernseed

could be *for to go invisible:* he'd sprinkle some
and be among tree-shades, near enough to touch the young deer
sniffing at celandine and bracken, pawing the fallen needles
till the word *ardent* puffs up like dust, along with
I cannot imagine life without you, although it has already
happened, staunch and solid as any grooved trunk

grappling the under-earth to it with arms of steel
for at least a century, a span in which their own firefly light
is a moment's matter, the merest glimmer gone—as they are
in this cloud of wailing dust and dear wounds aching,
whose mother tongue is silent and scold, is no, is yes.

Up Against It

It's the way they cannot understand the window
they buzz and buzz against, the bees that take
a wrong turn at my door and end up thus
in a drift at first of almost idle curiosity,
cruising the room until they find themselves
smack up against it and they cannot fathom how
the air has hardened and the world they know
with their eyes keeps out of reach as, stuck there
with all they want just in front of them, they must
fling their bodies against the one unalterable law
of things—this fact of glass—and can only go on
making the sound that tethers their electric
fury to what's impossible, feeling the sting in it.

Bonnard's Mirror

Vehement spices, a prodigal fog of them.
Lightning flashing its albatross wings,
thunder coming to rattle their bones. Then

the still small voice of the perfume she wore
is beating its tiny flourescent fists
and turning him inside out again, his eyes

on the figure fixed in the painted mirror,
framed and then framed again
with her head missing. A ripe brown berry

centres the swell of the breast, a line
slides from one nipple down her side
and shadowed thigh—shadowdark thickening

where both thighs must touch each other.
Seeking anywhere to settle, his gaze falls
on what's painted outside the glass: a jug

and basin; bathroom bottles, scents, ointments:
a tiled still life where she might still
be standing among soaps, toothpaste, perfume,

and not losing her head at all
but giving him, caught in the picture with her,
the full force of her open smile

and the matching candour of her body,
the lithe, droplet-glinting quick of it,
as if she'd rise and fly if he didn't hold her

there in the show they've made of themselves—
twinned and stilled like that for a flash
in the looking-glass, but feeling the real light

light on bare heads and steaming shoulders.

Pulse

Headier than anything distilled or fermented,
shudder-touch of the pulse between her legs
with his flat-open hand on it, taking its small beats
as they tumble after one another one by one,
as a bird inside a hiding place of wet leaves
might give the game away, the whole branch
a spasm asperging suddenly air with light-drops,
silence broken by a faint cry of fright as a hand
bunches and pushes in—fingers bent, extending
their search for softness, wild eyes igniting
as it backs deeper into the dark till it can no more
and in a commotion of flesh and feathering feels
pulse against pulse, and capture, coming to light, release.

In the Dunes

When you close your eyes in such a silence
death could come up behind you like an old friend
on tiptoe and touch you and that's that, goodbye
the world. I keep my eyes shut fast in this pure nothing

where sand and hedges are still in no wind at all
(almost a miracle on this sea-rounded tip of things)
and hear nothing at first, nothing, and then—as if
out of the egg of silence—small sounds hatching:

thin fluting of a goldfinch; song sparrow's single note
of warning; in the distance a hawk's cry broken off;
crackle of one twig slipping free of another; the tide's
perpetual faint susurrus, no end to its run-on sentence,

and that dry whisper as the sand in sleep keeps shifting.

Anti-Psalm

Where not so much as dreams of light may shine,
Nor any thought of greenness, leaf or bark.

—HENRY VAUGHAN, "THE TIMBER"

Big transit of clouds, small transit of birds through the garden.
        Beside the neolithic stones a post transporting electricity.
Then turn that last corner and there it is again: a sea of light.
        And still the world looking back, speaking in tongues,
and a few windows open in the grass, there, under my eyes
        outside my window, windshaken as I am
inside a local corner of the weather, reading psalms. Sunday morning:
        no coffee, no oranges, but a fry of rashers, eggs, sausages,
and the broken coast-lights weathersmacked. I might be standing yet
        beside the empty phone-box, sound of the heart in my mouth
a steady racket, balking again from nearness,
        warm of one cheek against the warm of another.
Constant this turning away: away from the withered hand,
        the eyebrows of malice, the widow's morning sickness,
the splinter-ache called daughter at the tip of my tongue.
        But elsewise: quick curl of smoke, a breath, and in the dust
at my bare feet a little pile of words—feathers that rise and fly
        with the next breath, a century or so later.

At Work

On slow wings the marsh hawk is patrolling
possibility—soaring, sliding down almost to ground level,
twisting suddenly at something in the marsh hay or dune grass,
their autumnal colours snagging his eye
where he finds the slightest aberration, any stir
that isn't the wind's, and abruptly plunges on it.
Then,
if he's lucky—and that scuttling minutiae of skin and innards,
its hot pulse hammering, isn't—he will settle there
and take in what's happened: severing the head first,
then ripping the bright red strings that keep the blood in check,
then eyes, gizzard, heart, and so to the bones, cracking
and snapping each one—that moved so swift and silent
and sure of itself, only a minute ago, in the sheltering grass.

White Water

Yes, the *heart aches,* but you know or think you know it could be
indigestion after all, the stomach uttering its after-lunch cantata
for clarinet and strings, while blank panic can be just a two-o'clock
shot of the fantods before afternoon comes on in toe-shoes
and black leotard, her back a pale gleaming board-game where all
is not lost though the hour is late and you've got light pockets.

There is a port-hole of light at the end of the hemlock tunnel:
birds cross it, flashing their voices at you, and you feel—
from the way they tilt their heads and their throats swell—
the beat of their brief song, another sign the world is what it is:
a shade-tree heavy with households, its fruit for meat, its leaf
for medicine. But that business of the first kiss is hard to fathom:

knees quaking, white water over broken rock, and the coracle
you trusted your life to in a bit of a spin, head swimming
with the smell of flesh so close you feel it breathing, spilling secrets—
its inmost name, for one, and what the near future feels like, time
wobbling to a tribal thing without tenses, and that tenacious "I"
a thing of the past, only a particle of the action now, nothing

separate, *a luminous tumult,* an affair of air and palate, air
and larynx, tongue, throat, teeth, whatever brings the words out
in their summer dresses—and you can hear the crow's black
scavenger guffawing, egg- and offal-scoffer, comedian of windspin,
so all of a sudden you rush your kingdom-come, the two of you,
insects shedding your dry, chitinous skins. And although what's left

is raw for a while, the slightest breath burns it, in time it comes
to become you, you can live into it, intoning the Sebastian koan—
whose who in pain? who's who?—and know, or close-to-know,
the *here it is:* two clean rooms in the next parish to wholeness.

Killing the Bees

They'd been there for years, secreted in the ceiling
of the back bedroom—between sealed rafters, plaster
and roof boards—making their own music, leading
a life blind to all but their native needs
and cycles. It couldn't last: armed, masked
under a cloud of sacking-smoke, we knocked a hole
into their cells, sowing anger and panic, a sound
we had, amazed, to shout over, masses of bodies
blackening the light-bulb, a live stalactite of honey
spiralling gold to the floor, the fumes we sprayed
killing them in their thousands. What survived
we dragged outside, drenched in petrol, put a match to,
dug a pit for. Bedroom a battlefield, bodies thick in it.

Vermeer, My Mother, and Me

Roof and sky and chimney stacks,
the blue, the white, the reddish browns—
how he might have seen Westfield Road
and the coppergreen spires of Mount Argus
from the window of my childhood bedroom

I can gather from a little corner
of his *Little Street,* and the almost
unremarkable presence in it
of the woman bent over in her own back yard,
who is leaning for a mop in a wooden bucket

and who just might be my mother
at our kitchen door, her eyes cast down
to the shore that's clogged and stinking again
as she takes in a breath—filled
with the smells of grass and apples,

coal dust, Jeyes Fluid, and the sugary
toffee scent from the factory down the road—
that will, when she raises her head,
come out with my name on it, my own
two syllables making their instant way

back through the kitchen, along the narrow hall,
up the dark-carpeted stairs and into
the small, wallpapered, big-windowed bedroom
where I'll hear that name and her known voice
shaping it, making it quick, making me

be there, myself in the very moment
when our daily life—defined

by cloud-broken blue sky and the ginger
bricks of gable-ends, radiance of roof-tiles
and wet chimneys—has to happen, there

where she's calling me to come, quick, help her.

Caterpillar and Dancing Child

It isn't only the child in the head it is,
but this one who dances her life for us—
turning like a miniature pillar of fire
before us, spinning on the tip of her toes
and spinning, taking the milk to the kitchen.
Or who'll float one step at a time
up the stairs to bed, or pirouette in the mirror
to see how her hair is, translating her life
into such speechlessness, full of herself
and the joy of it, moving, moving,
or who'll open our ears, amazed, to the sound
of her singing a hymn of angel-bread
in Latin, till the house fills with it,
the bread flies from the table,
and the flowering crown-of-thorns in the corner
twists light into itelf, as if in scarce earth
it could live forever—forever bright-eyed
in this house of cards where the cat
is scooped up by a small pair of arms
and forced close to our hearts.

Yesterday

I missed by inches crushing a caterpillar
underfoot in the spring-lit garden: exact
as a Japanese lacquered box, it was
black-bodied, fringed, white-streaked,
with tiny turquoise eyes on its flanks
and legs the colour my beard was once,
and I watched it ripple through grass-stems,
driven by the one leaf that speaks
to its hunger, where it eats its fill, then flows
over a wilderness of grit, bright mica morsels
marking its way—not at the speed of light
but in the arms of it, putting one foot

in front of the other, and covering
the ground as we do—towards that
deep undreaming sleep in which
it will become, as our child is, a life dancer.

Rainbow Skirt

Between bars of rain, the table looks out at the bird.
        Wrapped in its own watershawl
the house is pecked at. So the tree comes down.

Days later, limbs lopped, it is a cold blaze
        of amputations—stacked neat as stanzas
in the mist and rain. Terminal spark of sap and sawdust.

Cedar waxwings stop in the top branches. Sit for a slow
        sun-polish to every feather. Lisping music, sipping
sunlight: hordes of small birds hurrying south.

In January—unimaginable!—two bluebirds. Day and night
        he is eating his knuckles
as if there were no tomorrow. Months mooning by. Years.

Sweat-speckled, honeyed at every pore—joined like any other
        couple at the hip. The etymology of grief
seeps into stones that hold the house together.

Crown of gold, rainbow skirt: "She doesn't say anything,"
        says the child, drawing Aphrodite. Paperwhite narcissi
rising from a rack of white stones. Hawk-light. Wind

cuffing water. Lightness of hands, blue veins pencilled in.
        Silver bangle, oxblood boots, bones
of the face: she's all there. *Forget your life. Get up.*

But not yet dawn in her golden, open sandals.

Encounter

The lake that was caked ice is ice no more,
but waves scudding and making foam, although
if you plunged your arm in up to the elbow
you'd touch the hard table-truth of ice, under which
brown trout tell their own story. A man with a gun

patrols the shore: be not a woodcock or a snipe
this rainy afternoon, or—if you are—sit still as stone
while his spaniel noses the drenched heather. Still,
he says, he'd never shoot a pheasant, *For aren't there
only a few about, the lovely creatures.* We stand

for a cigarette, his gun cracked open, and in his hand
two cartridges of shot (wine-coloured, with gold
bands closing them) lie, like matching rings.

Agnostic Smoke

Open daisies in the grass, stars in the sky, that half-barrel
and the birds on it, or the silvery steely slateblue skin
of a mackerel: honeycomb of spiderlines and diamonds
and inside in close-up—look!—royal blue. Where do birds go
nights, or buff-colored heifers up to their bellies in buttercups
as they haul as if nothing the great weight of themselves
to lake edge and back, sinking beyond their bony hocks
in the boggy grass, the brushed green rushes making
a sound like raincoats? Nothing but blues of space waiting
my agnostic praise, but from my chimney, too, lord,
the smoke goes up, though this is after rapture,
and the sight of a pheasant crossing the morning garden
briskly, like a man on business, can't trigger whatever
the celebratory nerve was—it's only the eye just looking
as a tree might look, intending nothing beyond
being there, breaking daylight into little brilliant bits
to become itself in every instant: barked, branched, alive
with leaf-light: countless its ways of being, being like that.

Bonnard's Reflection

His bedrooms reek of sex and melancholy:
whose leg flexes over a shoulder, whose
hot hand finds a thigh, arms around
the smooth swerves of whose back? We clutter,
he says, and choke. We fail love,
telling all sorts of lies. The whole pink globe
of the cherry tree pressed against one window,
blotting the sky out. Eros erodes us. This
is where itch begins to rhyme with ache:
one more nail in whose coffin? You'll wait
and see. Flowers on the down comforter
already hissing and whispering what it is
they know to the flowers on the dawn curtain.

Shock Waves

Sunflower seeds, stone walls, eyes in hiding, phantasmagoria
of the sighted world: I wear white dunes in my eardrums

and it's no world I hear, not even a lust-muffled last echo
when the chambers open and shut, shaking the walls, the boat

of words rising on these shock waves, rising and falling, I feel it
but hear no syllable of the slipslapslop of agitated ocean

across the bow, nor the long telegraph of blue notes that the huge
underwater heart-stoppers use to wreak erotic havoc, each

to each, not the least beat heard where the green bent of branches
and the frantic signing of hemlock to cottonwood

point peremptory directions. *Be,* they sign me; then, *Be other,*
in that *long viduity* of aura, when even breathing—its heavy

spondees measuring the night—disappears, becomes another
nothing in the world, though the soundless heart, celled

in hush like honeybees sleeping, still does
what it has to (composing itself in a constellation of shades)

and stays for a sign out of your small hands, now the enamel-
skinned Adriatic is cracked behind us, the air frothy

and wide-awake with longing, the hard clear stars saying the way.

After Rain

See how our big world turns tiny and upside down
in raindrops on thorns of gorse: along the lane
to the small harbour the hedges are empty of leaves
and everything has a flayed, scrubbed look, antique
and about to be new, the brusque wind flailing branches,
declaring change, a change in the weather
that must unsettle us, too, who persist inside its loops
and mazes, unable to see straight, unable to forecast
tomorrow or the day after, only able to remember
what happened: the air scenting to freshness, a sense
of calm coming down, of getting to the other side
of turbulence, of things being touched for once
to wholeness, that somehow nothing bad could happen.

With Skeleton and Shoes

White ticking of the cricket in the grass. Companionable
answering. Two whispering like that as long as you can listen.

Gull skeleton filling with sand: ribcage a basket of bone and air
to keep a cricket in, or a green grasshopper with cinnamon legs.

Fluctuant cloud, your blood, the drift of a woman's thighs
crossing a corridor in the opposite direction. Too late for eyes

or faces: the rest is famine. In a darkness full of stars and children
you're learning the names: fairytales of design where there is none,

although immediately we see it. Smears of light. Sensualities
of shade. Heart of cloud is limestone, its rim brightness.

Whole day in front of the window watching wind-driven birds:
the way the grass, the leaves, are nodding and touching.

Today the wind, southeast, has warm hands—hundreds of them
laying about you, surprising skin and bone. Remember

how things were inhabited? Learning the word made flesh, meeting
Vincent's Franciscan shoes. Dazzle-amber of the shirt you wore,

and dusk a breathing field of cows: body language of mother and child—
muzzle nuzzling neckflap; quick bright flesh-flash of tonguelick.

Wind Chimes

Thunderhead. Thundercloud.
First a hush in which
the persistent small voices grow
querulous in their immense
present instant, agitated,
waiting for it.

—

Weeks no sign of the moon
although she's there, buried
above clouds, getting on
and on with her changes.

—

The feel of fingerbone
when hands are joined
like that and folded: small
flushed hands, olive-mottled.
And going to the door
at intervals: is that thunder?

—

Drying, things get lighter,
dreaming flight. Look—
it is evening; look,
she said, it is nearly night.
And *A kiss on the head*
wipes away memory. Meaning,
she meant to say, it didn't.

—

Now birds sing on little
quiverbranches in my skull
and the manic lark

lights out of my ear
in somersaults of song
where my eyes, God rest them,
are flying. So things
may start to look back at me:
the barrel, the sheep's horn,
even the lake, the reeds, even
the spade, earth-clotted,
leaning against hedge-glow.

—

Tomorrow, too, will be
the verb 'to miss.' How it
prises between skin
and skeleton, swims
quick rivulets of blood,
figuring even the way
fingers clutch the pen.

—

But what is it keeps
the voice in check?
One foot, it is,
nailed to the bedroom floor.
There it goes again—
that silence. So
open your mouth. Spell
'branks.' Close slowly now.

Country Road

Scarlet mask, copper wings: to be wakened from a dream—
        a woman singing Mozart's *Requiem*—by the dawning
cockcarracarouse of the anemone-cheeked bird
        shouting his foreign heart out. Two fried duck eggs
stain my plate to a painter's palette: deep golden yolk
        drawing fire from the window. Meantime the day
grows porous, turning light inside out, into a shade
        with no name, the way someone may paint a hedge
of blackberries or a narrow country road that's empty
        except for this momentary slanted light, with mulberry-
coloured roof-tiles in the distance. Mid-afternoon
        and nothing there, and he paints it into his journal of loss:
matte grey sky, black evergreens, water-gloss—all
        a backdrop only. Now the longest day
is closing down: a bat-breath brushes my hair; a blackbird
        dashes jabbering at the garden. In this big
wing-spreading silence, little to believe, less to hang onto—
        simply different registers of grass and tree bark, hedges
dimming, a glimmer of gravel, and the sky like
        faded rice paper. Relax, she says, and take in if you can
these drenched buttercups, dripping fuchsias,
        even the rain with that seeming sourceless glow
inside it. But take nothing for granted, not even this
        North African orange that sends its own probe
of sunshine into the cloudy room, scorching
        the walls. So, when the weather is—as it mostly is—
wet and windy, I'll stay indoors over a book, leaning
        closer and closer as light dwindles, to scan it
by that peculiar sheen of rain-light and leaf-light
        and stone-light leaching through the big window.

Landscape with Teeth

Cattle dusk-sculpted on a plinth of skyline.
Breast of chaffinch a watered strawberry.
Caher Island a whale-shape on the glazed sea.

Bog, clod, soggy, sod, plod. Nimbus
of light over boggy pasture; couchgrass
in flattened mats; blunt push of mushrooms

through loamy hush. Nests, passage graves,
crosses. Steam-clouds out of the cows'
rosy mouths. Soft furnaces of their body-bulk.

Three girls moving through rainmist
under a huge blue umbrella, waiting for Monet
to paint them as they are on the headland:

grey swell of sea, horizon a pale lapis, the sky
chequered with cloud; a pointillist silvering
shiver of rain. Their poppy-coloured laugh.

Indoors, a window-ledge of books, that umber
Italian vase of meadowsweet and loosestrife,
a spray of fuchsia against the verdigris

and plumblue bulges of Tully Mountain.
In the foreground one rusted sickle, a single
blip of sunlight igniting its bent tip.

But where do the real dreams come from
in their primary colours—with their small teeth
pointed, and their warm wet tongue?

Detail

I was watching a robin fly after a finch—the smaller bird
chirping with excitement, the bigger, its breast blazing, silent
in light-winged earnest chase—when, out of nowhere
over the chimneys and the shivering front gardens,
flashes a sparrowhawk headlong, a light brown burn
scorching the air from which it simply plucks
like a ripe fruit the stopped robin, whose two or three
cheeps of terminal surprise twinkle in the silence
closing over the empty street when the birds have gone
about their own business, and I began to understand
how a poem can happen: you have your eye on a small
elusive detail, pursuing its music, when a terrible truth
strikes and your heart cries out, being carried off.

FROM *The Quick of It* 2005

because the body stops here because you can only reach out so far because the pointed blade of the headache maps the landscape inside the skull and the rising peaks with their roots behind your eyes their summits among the wrinkles of your brow because the sweat comes weeping from your hands and knotted nipples because your tears keep kissing your cheek and your cheek feels the tip of another's tongue testing your tears because the feel of a beard along the back of a neck is enough to melt the windows in a little room because the toes the thighs the eyes the penis the vagina and the heart are what they are and all they are (orphan, bride, pheasant or fox, freshwater glintfish of simple touch) we have to be at home here no matter what no matter what the shivering belly says or the dry-salted larynx no matter the frantic pulse no matter what happens

So this is what it comes down to? Earth and sand
Skimmed, trimmed, filletted from rocky bone, leaving only
Solid unshakeable bottom, which won't in the end give in

To the relentless hammer, whoosh, and haul-away of tides,
But stands there saying, *Here I am and here I stay,* protestant
To the pin of its terminal collar, refusing to put off the sheen

Of its sheer-scoured surface, no widow weeds in spite of loss
After loss, whole wedges of the continent, particles of the main
Plummeting from one element to the other and no going back

To how things were once, but to go on ending and ending here.

A morning washed to gleaming skin and bone, to the vapoury radiance left
By rain, to such absolutes as my own shadow burnt in tree bark and hedge leaf,
Living its other life there while I walk its present provisional body towards

The vanishing point, peering back to see a small fleet of ducks muckraking
The grassy verge—for earthworms, I guess, whose thirst has brought them out
To savour the aftermath of last night's downpour, blind blood-coloured bodies

Sliding through raptures of damp, through the palpable slow ecstasies of drip
And slobber, smells of freshened earth their paradise as the ducks peck at
And swallow morning's manna—a gift to give thanks for in an anthem of quacks

As they waddle a swamp of sunlight—totally for the moment and at home in it.

With a little quick shudder the bushes part and offer to my eyes a wren

That stops there, seeming entirely intent on the strains of Mozart's
Symphony 29—composed by a boy in love with Italy, as the wren's
Coal-speck eyes are in love, it would seem, with that splash of light

Brassing the grass, and with the scarlet dazzle-dangle of a fuchsia skirt
With purple lining. It is that nib-specific *focus* I'm seeing in the bird
And hearing in the music, the in-lit contingent presence things hold

In the moment to moment passage of their happening, the wholehearted way
They're in a state made up of bristling force and chaste patience—which
Stars have, and wind-twisted sycamore leaves, and the seeds of lightning.

Back they sputter like the fires of love, the bees to their broken home—
Which they're putting together again for dear life, knowing nothing
Of the heart beating under their floorboards, besieged here, seeking
A life of its own. All day their brisk shadows zigzag and flicker

Along a whitewashed gable, trafficking in and out of a hair-crack
Under wooden eaves, where they make a life for themselves that knows
No let-up through hours of exploration and return, their thighs golden
With pollen, their multitudinous eyes stapled to a single purpose:

To make winter safe for their likes, stack-packing the queen's chambers
With sweetness. Later, listen: one warm humming note, their night music.

Deep as it might be, what is our silence to the silence of the village of Slievemore,
Its upstanding stone skeletons open to the blows any booming weather off the ocean
Can throw, its grassed lanes and main street given over to the air since hunger

Struck, laying them low, hunting the shawled and barefoot villagers onto the road
Towards the boat at Louisburgh, the long haul to Newfoundland or South Boston,
Their old home a haven now for gulls, a hawk or two, some gannets plummetting

Among the rocks, who'll weather there, sitting out the storm's ferocity? And what
Is the little edgy chill that lingers between us to the great freeze that folded snow
And cliffs of ice over most of the island, though it left one corner free to be itself—

So strange shapes of land and stranger flowers settled there and became native?

Bent over his time-polished pitchfork, my neighbour who's turning hay
In the big wind blowing off the Atlantic is the moving hieroglyph
For *Man-who-belongs-here* or *Two-hundred-years-ago,* which is also

The sign of a local tree, the sycamore baring its pied bark and giving
Leafy tongue to the air's passage through it, that long run-on sentence
Trembling toward its final verb which can be days coming, during which

One invisible blackbird goes on making music, becomes an inky swirl
On shadow-paper, a sounding heart in the heart of uproar, a brushed text
That would say, could we see it, *High wind: morning all tossed about—*

His incendiary yellow-ringed eye running rings out to the rings of Saturn.

Casual, prodigal, these piss-poor opportunists, the weeds
In their gladrags and millennial hand-me-downs
Of yellow and purple and pale green, squat everywhere
Along the highway, on every inch of waste ground
In our cultivated suburbs where they raise their families

And squinny through lace-curtained windows, wagging
Their heads at us, flaunting their speechless force, their
Eager teeming in themselves, the irresistible fact
That theirs is the kingdom, the power, and the glory
Of the real world smiling full and frightful in our faces.

Off the skin of water scumbled blue a ghostly steam-mist rises, as the frost-
Chilled air kisses river surfaces and something changes. Something changes
When two outsides touch like that, each sensing the touch of that sudden other,

As something changes when our wrists and fingers settle and slowly stroke
Each other, taking time to savour the way we feel what's happening here:
The cool of skin meeting the under-heat that blood is, and answering

Its delicate imperative with this smoulder-burn, this elemental shift from
Earth to air and what begins to feel like fire, as if a ghost of soul shimmered
Above the skin we share, the way those wavering radiant exhalations now

Curl their incessant ghost-shapes off the skin, air-kissed, of river water.

A summer of blackened slats, murder of bees, stale perfume,
And in the dripping leaves off-stage where you wait to go on
There is this low whimpering. But when you have done some
Small thing—filled the feeder to brimming with millet and sunflower,
And a chickadee hops near your disappearing thumb and perches
And proceeds to eat, and the zip of daylight hisses on wingflicker,
And a bell sounds from God-knows-where and it's nothing you know
And gone sooner than it takes to say *This happened—*

still it did,

You know it did, you felt whatever it was, and even the weight
Of that past tense can't quench the quickened life it had in it.

Quick now, it's as if air had bared its bright teeth: snow petals
Blowing so everyone stops to stare a minute at the last flitters
Of winter come among us, then sun again, as if the season's drunk

On its own manic fast forward—as a couple on bumpy ground
Will swerve between humours, their talk now fire, now ice; sunshine,
Then rain quickly following; cloud that in an instant clears.

But what are those creamy yellows breathing in and out at the end
Of maple branches? Haven't they heard? Are they deaf as posts—
And all their seed, breed and generation—to what happens here

Where we have to live, nature or no nature, keeping our own score?

Skelped, ice-bladed, fairly scarified by this gale with hail in its teeth,
You keep seeing the rainbow in the belly of the storm and you want

The work—though it won't be all things to all men—to have myriad
Instances in it: gale, hail, rainbow, the way these ice grains hop off grass

And how your cheek feels, being struck, not to mention the dark-headed
Running plover, the yellow petals of gorse that signal some new *now*

To grey, February-naked air, or the stream so over its stone causeway
It can't be crossed and you have to turn back the way you came, turning

The other cheek to hailstone and wind-nip, bearing the brunt of weather,
Learning what *storm of circumstance* really means, and *winds of change.*

Touch-me-not wherever I look—its tiny orange cup and spur curling or spitting seed
If I brush against its frail green stem while running myself into the ground here

Where students have begun to saturate the space again, their ripe bodies shining
From every corner, travelling singly, doubly, or in packs, their youth a raw burn

Against the season I feel in my depths: arms, bare legs, the way, like brazen water,
Slick shoulder blades and back muscles ripple, greased and made sleek by the clean

Sweat-film that gleams there. So I learn the cloud–lid on life, again, is *full of rifts*
Of glowing light, and may even lift to let through an eye-hooking slash of blue—

As a woman in a summer dress riding a bike will let the silk ride suddenly up
In no breeze but her own motion, and her thigh is alight there where your eyes are.

When a heron, that protected bird, and a windhovering hawk appear
Framed in the one window for a minute, as the bigger slowly flaps
Towards Tully Mountain and the other does its Nijinsky trick of standing
On air—wings so fast they're like a long sentence out of Beckett, energy
Immensely expended on going nowhere, shaping up for the kill—I don't

Only remember the heron folding and unfolding itself over Omey Strand
When we spread your mother's ashes on the water and I said *An image
Of eternity* (though *patience* must have been what I meant), but think also
Of the small heart hiding in heather-tufts and hoping—breath by breath,
Smell by smell—for another instant free of those lethal eyes, then another.

What disappears when I say the word *bird?* That little thing all shades
Of brown and raspberry and rose on my windowsill: clicking bill, a feathering

That raddles light; depthless black reflecting eye; a syncopating bulge where
Heartbeats harry the breast; the swifter-than-eye-can-follow side to side flick

Of the head? I can hear its distinct twittervoice. *Finch,* I say, getting
A hold of it. *House finch.* It doesn't move a muscle. Then a branched robin

Fan-batters charcoal wings, and I see before it disappears its burnt-orange
Breast, an ember blown to brightness by the cloudy morning, and I almost

Feel it as the quick blink of God's one eye, the eureka-brisk surprise given
And taken, the *echt* unmanageable absolute of it in the moment passing.

It must be a particular kind of grace, the way this wild morning a family of swallows
Is harvesting the cloudy air: harnessed to its wheels and pulleys, they harness

The blast to their own advantage, or stop on it for a second before letting its breath
Take them where it will, their small streamlined bodies abroad and at home

In its hugeness, their screams carried off so I can catch only the faintest trace
From where I stare out the kitchen window, wideawake to these tiny life bundles

In daily negotiation with the great unnameable force that lives in things, the way
They're beyond complaint, too busy living to be bogged or beaten down for long

By sudden swerves of weather; beyond even contentment; having only this instant
Quick knowledge the moment gives them: and how to go on, making the most of it.

When my daughter begins to talk logic, murmuring over and over such open secrets
As *Law of detachment, modus tollens* and *disjunctive inference* (the big words, it seems,

Making her mouth happy) I find we're standing on another threshold, and see
Her recede from me into the quiver-thicket of her own life, its zigzags hidden

So I can't follow her to the heart of where she's going, leaving me in the middle
Of this dark wood, though still in earshot of each other—so even if she won't see me

Here in a splash of accidental light, she'll hear the words I'm saying and the way
I say them over, getting them by heart, sending them after her into the distance

She's starting to be now, learning to be her own language, from where
She'll send back bulletins (reports, coded probes, quick proofs) to find me.

While I'm hanging out this bath-towel, colour of blackcurrant and claret, it flaps
Like a prayer-flag, bringing back the sunbursting gale that blew the three of us
Out of Mannin Bay and into the grassy dune where we lay to picnic on salted
Tomatoes and the finer salt of sand in the cheese sandwiches, and heard the wind

Clatter across rocks between us and the shoreline, and felt safely tucked away
Until Kira made me stand on a steep rise and hold between us the big towel
Swelling like a spinnaker, madly crack-dancing, a live sail trying to take us with it

Though we stayed—unsteady on the edge as we were—grounded and holding our own
Against the weather, its pitch and fling and drag snatching our laughter but leaving us

Half air-creatures, and you reclining there like a sand-nymph, one weather eye open.

Rained in all day like this, I keep towelling the windows dry,
Trying to wipe the fog away that has me blind behind glass,
Unable to see the world outside for what it is, how things

Become shadows and blunted silhouettes of themselves, birds
Only blurs where they shake a branch when they land or leave
Or just dash past, a flash of cloud-particles snatching at crumbs

As I do myself each time I get the big window clear again and try
To take in all the shapes and colours there, all those living bits
Of matter that stand in their own ordinary uncanny light

Until blearing begins again, and I see my own breathing does it.

Good to draw the rake through cut grass: dry wisps catch in the plastic
Yellow tines, make a scratchy sound as they gather and you shake them off

And reach for another rakeful, your movements slow, deliberate, steady
As rowing. Good when the live grass comes up clean and green, and you see

The neatness of it, how it shines, starting life again in the free air, letting
Light stroke every slick blade, sleek-shining from its time in the dark:

Caught between satisfactions of rhythm, sound and sight, you see this is how
What you want to say may come clear as you revise (raking the dead away,

Bringing the living to light), till you find under a tuft of cut grass a wild bees' nest
Which you cover again, having seen its tiny golden honey-eggs blaze by daylight.

As if on cue, the heron's a rising and gliding apparition, casting no shadow
On the packed snow I'm running over, morning under cloud a dull grey
Ache. Frigid air's taken in at the mouth, to mix with the warm world
Of tongue and palate, gums at blood heat: it informs with its *frisson* of chill

The spongy honeycomb of lungs, and lives a few expansive instants there
Before turning like a swimmer and journeying back and out into frosted air
As a quick wisp of steam, the sign of my being here and now—as that heron
Tilting between branches is here and now, taking air in and letting it out

As he angles through it and over the rise and out of sight, seeking a safe
Still fluent place to feed in peace, before this cold un-homes everything.

When I see the quick ripple of a groundhog's back above the grass, its earth-

Brown pelt vanishing into a hedgerow which for a minute or two is a shaken

Screen of greens and then again still, the creature melted into nature's mouth

And sending back no sign of itself

though I know it's in there and I can sense

How its breath and the broadly distributed embrace of its gaze have become so fully

What it inhabits it will even winter there, curled round its own heart beating

At quarter speed, at ease in the sphere of its own immediate knowings, then

For some reason Avon's native comes to mind—quill-end tipping his tongue

As he takes a breath and disappears into the leaves and lavish music of another

Turbulent little word-shiver for a minute, and he is all alone there, listening.

All his life, we're told, *Chardin struggled to overcome his lack of natural talent,*
So I begin to look again at his olives and peaches, at that cut-open cantaloupe
With its orange innards on show, or that orange from Seville he kept giving
A bit part to—to burn softly in its given space, to weight the picture in a newly
Luminous way.

Or how the dead rabbit's fur is a dry gleam of white at the heart
Of warm browns, or the way each feather in the dead red partridge is a live thing—
The bird's life stilled to this final exposure of itself.

The struggle you see is with
The facts themselves, and with some knowledge he kept hidden from our eyes, some
Unspoken sense of how *there* these bodies are, and nothing can say it the way it is—

Only you look again, stretch your hand, dip the bristles, risk again the failing stroke.

FROM *Matter of Fact* 2008

What It Is

It is in the smallest leaf—of oak, maple, elm, dogwood, birch
or Chinese redwood. In the way leaves droop in the air
of this rain-laundered time of day, each involuntary drip
a pearl-drop earring. Shadows of barn gable and pin-oak tree
live in print on the avocado green of grass. What it is

is that *Amen* stuck in Macbeth's throat, or the road one
wheatear didn't take, or the child you didn't have the right
time or space to have, all its dark-eyed answers—eyes
glittering behind each twig of the persimmon, fleshlights
igniting every fruitglobe. What it is is ripening, so

inhale the immaculate late afternoon as you pass
through the garden: fruit, dust, moist fungus, a fine distillate
of finality you keep breathing, being in your own way
a part of it, wanting its laden air to leaven your lungs,
letting the heart be a small box of beaten gold that holds

secrets and hopeless promises. It is rife with promise.

Start of March, Connemara

(In memory of Elizabeth Bishop)

The wind colder even than March in Maine, though the same sea
is your greens of mutton-fat jade and bleached artichoke,
the water thumbed, wind-scumbled, its heroic white manes
blown to bits at the shoreline. Two white gulls, wing-tilted,
are surfing the sou'wester. How do they do it, finding the right
angle in the gale and—angels of the shiverblast—adapting to it,
letting it take them the way they're going?
A lone cormorant
blackly flashes, heading west like a messenger. Breasting
the choppy wave-peaks, he's all purpose and intensity, plunging
headlong into his own unknown future, reaching out to it
without a thought, while I go back the way I came
along wet sand that's glistening with relief, my own prints
erased already, *writ in water.*
Rock and water have to be
our elements here, and today's buffeting air—which these
rain-plovers pay no mind to, a little tribe rising as one, spinning
into the wind, whistling their shrill excitement in flight: glitterwings
making their mark against green gape-water, then gone.

Something

Something to do with how raindazzle at cloudbreak
touches up three apples in their skins and makes them blush
teal, cinnabar, gamboge; something with how that swan

stands splayed, a lovely alien, on slime-covered stones
at Claddagh-mouth; the cormorant speeding downstream
has something to do with it, taking advantage of the Corrib's

last mad dash for the sea, scattering black-headed, crack-
voiced gulls, keen gliders, eyes like needles in their search
for scraps, casual vigilantes of anything out of the ordinary

run of things on the river; and something about how
those clouds pack their massy granite granaries with light—
makes me ask what law in physics keeps these bottles

and bits of chipped wood in the turbulent trough
of the small waterfall spinning and spiraling, fleeing
in circles, going nowhere: however far they fling

themselves in the roil and roaring foamburst, they're
caught and drawn in, at once fugitive and centripetal,
stuck where they are while something in them seems

a big breathless thrusting out that won't give up
the struggle, though it avails nothing, simply brings all
back where it began, dizzy with longing, starting over

again, and again over again, as if it meant something.

A Few Facts

The chiming clock. The girl at her desk sneezing.
The hiss of traffic after rain has sleeked the street.
The chime sounding off the silent library air.
Outside, a kind of monumental after-icy-rain
relenting, something loosening and the ground
going soft, glistening, the water on it taking in
the world, the broad sycamore drawing water
up its roots, the huge trunk sopping it. In the room
the vase of Cremone daisies: yellow, white
and flaming orange. Shoes and books, a lit figure
bent to her work, lifting her shoulders slowly
up and looking out, letting a breath go. Smiling
when the child comes in with a question. Outside,
the spreading yellow maple shedding branches. A cairn
of bulky logs. Birds from dawn to dusk at the feeder:
black flashings across the blank window. The cats
dazzled, feeling the old hunger. Now the child
is posing, an arabesque, by the stove; now she's
wrapped in a rug, reading; now she is sitting up
in bed, a duchess, asking for her cardigan, grinning
at the laden tray—its porridge, milk, tea, striped napkin
in its ring—at light seeping through blue curtains.

Look Out

This morning it's our bare, moist, muscular masters, the trees, that have to stand in shadowy majesty for something. No stopping the colourstuff in pussy willows, or what happens to any stem this weather reddens, thickens, fills with only its own happening.

The needle pumping nothing through your tongue but pristine numbness has you waking around mid-day, sun blazing, dumb as a fish being filleted for tomorrow's dinner—not sole on the bone but some slow simmered thing that leaches all its life-juices out and sets them one against the other, to teach you again how in the end good ends depend on death to begin with.

Turning the other cheek is not the answer: didn't the shadow of the turkey vulture—itself a black shadow stapled to the blank blue sky-face—only yesterday cross the path you were tracing, and didn't your blood skitter for an instant, sensing its thwart and pitiless intention?

But could words like *relish, savour,* or *abide* strike a right note to end on? Now clouds are brazen radiance, are scarcely matter—only thick light, white brilliance against blue. Later they'll grow a heart-fraught leaden grey, day dimming—though a still fierce gleam to the west makes one small nimbus melting in the blue, transfiguring birches and leftover snow to this deep, meditative rose.

Another time it's a word like *roofbeam* brings you out of emptiness: you picture the nestle of it, light smearing its grain, the long silence before sleep, your father finding a fresh unclouded residence in the offing—a sort of guardian, different, kissed, beyond reliable.

Then sleep makes a clean sweep of things, the ceiling of your head a crown of stars, their names unknown, a realm away from impermanence—though that's your main address now, the word *home* cropping up only here and there. Because—as the maker of mists remarked that first morning—*Love is not consolation, it is light.*

Innocence of Things

Driving north. Shivers of valediction.
Tweed-folds of the Catskills in abrasive light;
risen flame of a redtail riding a thermal;
two geese through blue immensity. Sun

scribbles its calligraphy of angle-spines
and snag-arms. All the dead leaves
up again, jigging and reeling from
this brash wind scatter. The barred

tail of a raccoon shimmers a little
in breeze-flutter. Rest of him sprawled
still as stone on the road's shoulder.
Drip of fresh meltwater off a snowbank

is the tick of the clock this March day
moves to, slow as moss-ooze. Brazen
daylight; acres of snow under a sky
of sapphire; and I'm remembering

my old friend's fine old hands
as she held the fork steady, snail-slow,
tendering a curl of baby corn
to her mouth, and I want to set her

next to the innocence of things
as they stand up in frailty and fortitude
to light, and take its daily measure—
their secular selves singular and glowing.

(In memory of Phoebe Palmer)

Breath

Small paws in leafmatter. Smell of resin and balsam filling me for a minute
before I go. All that's alive in this necropolis of wanwood and woodchip
is the scent of what was locked deep in leaf-vein and the grain of things

when the woods were walk-through and see-about, where now two squirrels
swirl skittering up peeled treebark. To stop in the middle of it all, the after-
noon light informing each crevice of bark, each filament in the squirrel's tail,

or gilding every mint-green smear of lichen, or falling like a tongue of fire
on a skyblue plastic canister—is to stand inside the pharmacopoeia of aromas
exhaled by mounds of rot, their airy liberated nothings become something

like that evidence of the world which I saw this morning in the small
bursts of breathsmoke out of a bluejay's mouth, the sign of the sound
of him standing on the feeder to make his own annunciation to the earth

he's the present epicentre of, and to me halted on its rim, hardly breathing.

City Dusk

Next door to the video store and the tattoo artist, under
the rattle and thrum of rush-hour summer traffic
that paces day with bells, horns, sirens, you'll stay
among rooms your nerves are getting used to: light

comes in without knocking, remains till after nine,
leaving its shadow-selves six stories down and
pottering under plane trees towards that park bench
among bottles and long overcoats, listening

to the Litany of Our Lady of Misfortune: *Shadow of*
stumbling mothers, pray for us. Shadow of crumbled wits,
pray for us. From this window, watch evening
fray slow to rose tatters, rags of cloud, a whisper

of mint green suddenly coming through. Soon
the time for words will lay its cool fingers to the skin
of your neck and waken the warm there, so you'll rise
as though from a dream, to find the room empty.

With Flowers and Curtain

Like lilies you imagine in the vestibule of Hell
these tall nameless flowers in front of the library

are straight talkers, blazing their rhetoric of *stare*
and *go away,* huge scarlet vowels setting minds on fire

with thoughts of furnace sex: to be just burned up
and no release. Is there no way to close your eyes

to such feral, fiery erections, shut out the sight
and not panic? Though your dreams are blood-soaked,

you wake dry as a bone to watch the bedroom curtain
dancing, its bulge and bellying and sudden intakes

making a waist, a hip, a hot flank on the go, an opening—
though you know it's only the wind getting wind of things

and leading its shaky life in any pliable, light, near-
alive object. But what body language it has:

no loop repeated, no gesture wasted, every shiver
melting into a next quickening shudder, the next

astonished full stop. Pause—then the garbage truck
is grinding the early hour into a hash of crashes, a clamour

of metal, glass, recyclable plastic. Wrenched towards
day-state by the woeful din of it, you have to think

how by the darkened library those flowers are burning
to a stalk; while the curtain, you see, is still dancing.

Another Week with Hölderlin

But where is the man
Who can remain free
His whole life long, alone
Doing his heart's desire?

Monday

Woods a green blaze; smoke off the lake. River-bowl of burning light. To be on, as he says, *roads travelers take.* World a wall of fire, boundaries between this and that eliding like light off harried water. In the underground, smears of firelight glisten at first from rusted tracks until—blind as beetles hearing the agony of shunt and wheel-shaft, the grind, the groaning—we start hauling the huge intractable weight of our *(what's the word?)* along with us.

Tuesday

In the city I lose one thing after another: the car, my glasses, the house I've passed the evening in with friends, the friends. Entering the cathedral, I descend with two or three strangers to the crypt and we close the heavy door. We pull the bell-ropes anchored there. We spin the pulleys working the bells. Up as high in the tower as I can see, one bell then another starts swinging, ringing. Belling, we pull, we spin, shaking ancient walls. The ground's raw earth knobbled with stone and, barred behind us, the door. We're bound to this—to filling the world with sound. *Likewise,* he says, *mourning is in error.* Still no one comes.

Wednesday

The Grand Canal near Portobello Bridge. Light shaping itself in the wake that one duck makes on murky water. The place Italian, almost, as sunshine. Sun-disk shattering on the mallard's stippled shadow. Folds of the Fates in Stephen's Green. *But desire,* he says, *is foolish in the face of fate.* On pitiless patches of grass the girls clutch at the boys, and the boys in their panic of pride clutch back. And grapple to them, looking away.

Thursday

Whose head, neat as a hinged lid, lifts just above the eyebrows? Floats in a flood of sudden commuters flailing across the station hall? I fumble in one face after another. Whose two eyes stab with *I miss you more than I can say?* The heart, blood thumping, comes into leaf, feels the heat. How it licks and nibbles. A bite of something like surprise. *Often when you've barely given it a thought,* he says, *it just happens.*

Friday

Spirit or not, he says, one *must keep to the world,* so you are grass coming up from under the long sleep of snow, every touch of colour bleached out, and you lie there, feeling nothing but the weight lifted that's buried you for months, letting the good air get to you with its hundred subtleties of touch, its promise of something happening at last, even a breeze strengthening to storm, a rasp of dead leaves, scouring hail, the way rain drills deep its glitter-fingers. Flesh, then: its kinetic harking after something headlong and lighthearted as the weather shifts and air becomes a spectrum of blues you can see through—no one of them going to waste.

Saturday

The Pissarros have became dimensional again, so you enter and are at home in one of their empty houses, the one framed in a cage of birches at a blind corner. *Someone reach me,* he says, *a cupful of dark light,* so you stand under a spilling gutter, see fat fire-water splashing, feel the quickbright lick of tongues, so your bare head burns and your neck glints and shivers, as if you'd happened to stand in the way of a blessing otherwise intended. It lucidates you, moving to its proper end—lodging there, still quivering.

Sunday

You watch the deer stepping downhill to the pond: a mother and two young, they pace graceful and steady, looking about. You're in the presence—*near,* he says, *and hard to grasp*—and try to remember the lilies of the field, the transparent air you're up against. It is a sort of start: a faint thing, but like the smell of blood and its taste in your mouth, salt-sweet.

In Venice on My Father's Anniversary

When the long boat stopped in the dark
where I stood among the pillars of the old fish market,
I hesitated till it was loaded with souls
who stood for the crossing, then let them go—
each pressing a coin into the hand of the boatman
whose breathing I could hear and the splash of his oars
when he turned the craft and ferried over the dark stream
that small troop of voyagers. But when
the boat came back a second time
I too stepped in with those waiting
and handed over my obol and took my stand with care
so the vessel wouldn't shake or waver. Then I felt
the night air and the breath of air off water
swaddle me, and heard only the in and out of oars,
and felt the water shaking under us where we stood
in the bodies we had. But
when we stepped ashore on the other side
into what I thought would be strangeness,
I find myself in the place I'd just left
and start walking the known track once more.

Steam in Sunlight

So start with sex: the sight of birds at seed,
their urgency a sequin of fire in tiny eyes—
and in mine too, maybe, as I burrow in,
an eel of hot intentions, a wheel
of give and take, a whole cascade of hope
before that ache of restoration to the world
as is, history in all its homely features
and the hour later than we think, footsteps
measuring the way the child enters, tentative,
and slides between us.
                                        So then we three
are peeling clementines and the day starts
closing over my head, till I catch nothing
but its racket of traffic, loud voices
muffled, my own words sunk like stones
stuck in the under-mud.
                                        Bundled back
into the body-suit, shackled to the tick
of heart-clocks, I call back the steam I saw
in sunlight after my shower, the bathroom
a tankful of molecular grey radiance
staining the world with its own infinite,
quick, instant-by-glittering-instant
play of starting over, the road open.

Hawklight

1.

Hungry season. Hawk, redtail, lights a vacant maple:
brain one continuous shivery nail-rasp, scorching eyes
to ash. Small birds on the alert, air cacophonous

with scales and prattlings. Hawk throws head about:
readiness is all, all solitude and manic appetite. Stand-by
in silhouette, figuring such verbs as *Want! Be-here!*

Stopped, you'll see the sudden tilt of his gingery
black head, quick blink of an eye in which you'd spot
yellow iris, pupil black as soot, the moonless void

of lethal patience that knows *when-where* to strike
once in an explosion of bones and tiny eyes
brimming with blood, a cry swallowed, a breath

quenched—earthbound or native to the air. Another day
goes by, survived: hawkvoice moves up a notch,
filing sky to wildness: sharp ravel-song splaying entrails.

2.

Sudden, a plummet, the marsh hawk enters a hemlock
and stands, steadying himself, stopped not far from
my head, on a branch too thick to shake or sway much

so I can see the hook of his beak and the livid black
and yellow target-circles of the eye he turns on me—
a laser graiping my grounded bulk into the meltdown

his brain is. Stays there out of the crows' way
that heckle, harass: alert to every twig-snap, footstep
and the strung silence into which a squirrel's just crept

with stuttering pulse, to shiver there, sheltering. So
I learn how heart heaves, how flexed muscle keeps
leashing, unleashing in a book of feathers, how tongue

hisses *hawkstand! squirrelshiver! crowclamour! now!*

What Happened

Smoke

Out of the blue. Out of the blue sky. Out of the blue sky over Manhattan. Out of the blue. Steelsmoke. Glasssmoke. Cloudsmoke. Bodysmoke. Screamsmoke over the roar. Blacksmoke. Black. Quick as thought the news traveling. Gone. Guns in the air. *Murdered sleep.* In the sunshine. A helicopter heading south. Shadow-wings and shadow-blades slicing buildings, blacking our standing figures looking up. The quick of it passing into the blue. Wait for it wait for it wait for it: the names, pillars of smoke, broken altar, silence. Reel of names. No one not there. Dirty joke of a laugh. The news not yet. Maybe it will not have happened. Bee shadow over the open page: *blank, shadow, blank.* Sounds from the street: the traffic beginning again as it must. Turn the page, another, another. Allblank. From their camps and bunkers they watch. The big men in uniforms and suits are watching and the small masked men in waiting are watching. Smoke. Cloudroar of smoke on the screen. Rewind. Roll it again. Again.

Afterword (The teacher thinks about his students)

All they want is adequate speech. So we reach across the Great Plains of the classroom table, tripping over our words. It will never be enough. Eyes of the lost. Tears where one is looking at me, trying to speak. *What man, ne'er pull your hat about your brows.* When I draw down the blinds, a sky of rubble and smoke is swept away to nothing, a blank. I know this script. It beggars translation. *Dispute it like a man?* Syllable by syllable the story *(story!)* is coming out—of red headbands, box-cutters, plastic knives. A book (a *book!*) of simple instructions. Barking and barked, lovingly, yes, at one another. First this, then that, then the other, and we are *(praise Heaven!)* home. Poor eyes drowning and no one to ask. *Please is my name on your list it is my father no is there another list?* When the book is passed from hand to hand to hand it falls open at "Smoke." It hurts to squint through it. A grievous affliction. To imagine we might loosen our tongues. That we might go on. They've gone home now, hungry as fieldmice in February. In silence. Not one crumb of comfort among them.

Ladybird and Mother

Sunday air thronged to throttling with ladybirds
opening and closing their wings, tiny gold buttons
that click and zip and glisten in the gold of October
and land on any leaf or level stretch of grass
or hot brick simmering in the glare. You used to see them
one at a time, and there'd be a minute's rapture
over the blessing of good luck: you'd make a wish
and watch the diminutive creature stretch its wings
and lift off the kitchen windowsill and vanish
into the branches of our neighbour's apple tree.
But why this black-freckled red or yellow beetle
conveyed good fortune, your guess was as good as mine,
though we knew it was under *Our Lady's* protection,
one more leftover from the age of faith you still
lived in—its garden appetites (gobbling aphids)
making this six-legged carapace a seasonal benediction,
as it still is for farmers: a sign of health in green leaf
and blossom, auguring a fine spring, no one
wanting to bring down out of the innocent blue
the bad luck in killing one, cleaving the clear line
of connection spreading from all corners of that
coleopterous cradle-world to the two of us
crunching into a ripe pippin. It was our kind
of superstition: small enough to fit in a kitchen garden
and not needing—as scarab or scorpion needs—
the sands of Egypt or vasty veldts of Africa
to dazzle in. This very minute *(the luck of it!)* my west-
facing window has a dozen contemplative ladybirds
flickering in their Sabbath trance on it. And listen:
Come back, they're whispering, *and wish on us.*

What Matter

Does it matter, moon at full, that moonshine
comes streaming through the bedroom window—
a shower of mercury, luminous
in the early hours so the cats are wide-eyed
with anticipation, fretful at every whisper,
and we lie awake, counterpaned with light,
our thoughts free range, not to be tethered?

And does it matter that light, late afternoon,
makes every willow leaf, every mallard feather,
each bristling filament in the doe's freckled ear
show itself for what it is—a strand of *gold*
to airy thinness beat, a sort of spirit-tip to tug
us out of the big picture, put us in touch
with the far edge of things where the heart

has been in hiding, harking after what's taken
root there, distinct as dark-night starlight
but nameless, simply a glimmer of inscrutable
integrity, a way of standing to attention
for a second, tantalizing the eyes out of your head
with hope, till the opening closes over
and your eyes and all they fall on

are only blunt, colourless stone? Day after day
does it matter that the heart of the matter
in the heart's heavy, loving tussle
with what matters—to eye, ear, finger-ends,
to all the tidal turbulence of the senses—
may rest in, may indeed come down to, this
momentary unfolding to blind spots, blankness?

Steady Now

Although things vanish, are what mark our vanishing,
we still hold onto them—ballast against the updraft
of oblivion—as I hold onto this umbrella in a world of rain,

of heavy wet greens and greys dissolving into a new
atmosphere, an underwater dulled electric glow
off everything, the air itself drowning in it, breath

thickening, growing mould. Yesterday I felt the smell
of grass greeting me as across a great distance, trying
to tell me one good thing in an underglaze of memory,

some forgotten summer trying to speak its piece. It is
the way of things and it never stops, never calls a halt—
this knocking and dismantling, this uprooting, cutting out

and digging down, so tall oaks and honey locusts
are laid low and drop to earth like felled cattle, shaking
the ground we've taken a stand on as if it were a steady

establishment, a rock of ages to outface ruin itself, not
the provisional slippery dissolving dissolute thing it is—
which we have against all the evidence set our hearts on.

Fix

Spread of light: momentary
molecular bristle of it
over your skin: how it
scrambles matter, so we need
painters (Caravaggio, say)

to slow it down, come
to rest in things, helping them
grow single, distinct
in a blaze of shade—every thread
a mote amazed at being intact

and turning its back
on change. Otherwise
we're only passing through—
a bruised leg curving
from light to dark; a blur

of flesh against the blond
wood of a doorframe—
only the helpless exposure
of things in spacetime
if the painter's eye and hand

fail to fix them. *Fix* them,
meaning make them
as they are, meaning *Look,*
we're here too: a burst fig;
the harp-shape, heat-glazed,

of a cricket; the sorrowful
sympathy in the ram's eye

as he offers himself
next in line to the knife—
a cornflower sky brightening

that lambent, mild iris.

Opposing Forces

Even in this sharp weather there are lovers everywhere
holding onto each other, hands in one another's pockets
for warmth, for the sense of *I'm yours,* the tender claim
it keeps making—one couple stopping in the chill
to stand there, faces pressed together, arms around
jacketed shoulders so I can see bare hands grapple
with padding, see the rosy redness of cold fingers
as they shift a little, trying to register through fold
after fold, *This is my flesh feeling you you're feeling.*

It must be some contrary instinct in the blood
that sets itself against the weather like this, brings
lovers out like early buds, like the silver-grey catkins
I saw this morning polished to brightness
by ice overnight. Geese, too: more and more couples
voyaging north, great high-spirited congregations
taking the freezing air in and letting it out
as song, as if this frigid enterprise were all joy—
nothing to be afraid of.

A Thrush by Utamaro

Although it looks the picture of perfect balance, and although I'd imagined nothing could be steadier (yellow legs locked fast to the softer yellow of a bamboo stake), and envied its way—at once solid and light—of being in the world, in fact the bird only appears in the painting for its name, *komadori,* which means *to be unbearably troubled.* But then I see that what I was really admiring is the way its tenacious grip on things is sustained in spite of how the world of broken stake and bursting chrysanthemum blossom is going to bits around it, its unbearable trouble being borne and lived inside as the creature must live inside its own name, remaining upright against the odds and holding on to that long bamboo as though it were a flute, whose music might match the thrush's own woodnotes, songs raised over wreckage when the dust has settled.

Bee Fuchsia

At this first brief lull
in terrible weather
bees are back, each
entering headfirst
the upside-down open
nectar-heavy skirts
of wet fuchsia flowers
and seeming to stay
quite still in that laden
inner space, only
the smallest shudder
of the two together
when the bee-tongue
unrolls and runs
its tiny red carpet
into the heart
of what is no mystery
but the very vanishing
point and live centre
of the flower's instant
irrevocable unfolding,
then stillness again
while this exchange
(layer after layer of
dusty goodness lipped,
given) is taking place—
the flower flushed
and swelling a little,
the bee gently but
hungrily clutching.

The Search

It's the sheer tenacity of the clematis clinging to
rusty wire and chipped wood-fence that puts this
sky-blue flare and purple fire in its petals. To be
new in autumn, in mid-September, to be showing
yourself like that, naked as water under full moonlight:

something has to be good in such a world, in the talent
it has for lasting and coming back, in the way
it decorates our graves, our standing walls, our back
porches, and in the way the late bee lands
on its dazzle, walks the circumference of every petal

in some minor key of astonishment—drinking
the last of its sapphire wine. What takes shape
is a cellular sense of how the moment is jammed
to splitting with excess, each pod and sweet kernel
plumped to bursting with the brash simplicities

of contradiction, the child's tears watering the plant
that seems from a shrivel of bones to make itself
an azure conflagration, seeming to say, *There's*
always more to say. Language can be like that,
taking its stand on the driest, most barren space

of clay, asking only that we attend, behold it being
no more than being itself—*a Nothing /. . . blooming.*
And tonight the old man, your father, smiled twice:
once when he'd reached the sofa after the fifty-mile
shuffle from the hall door; once when his tongue

tasted the tart cool of a spoonful of blueberries
and he turned his eyes, shining their milky blue, on the child
who lifted her brimming spoon and smiled back at him.

(for Rachel)

Cold Comfort

Snow loosening its hair, letting it fall in streams,
snow that was knotted up with cold . . .
—PHILIPPE JACCOTTET, "MARCH"

The light dying and you look back at it. *Now,*
she said, *he is a god of glimmer,* meaning Apollo
or some other deity of desire and motion. Odd

that in the inexpressible inside, the tenanted void
of the center, you can recognize but put no name
to the way you are yourself, only feeling it

in the instant of its disappearing: smoke-bubbles
of breath on a cold morning. You are not
what you were, but between one blink and another

something in you knows how it was, knowing
Being for what it is, and is no more. My mother
would put it more simply: *To air,* is what she'd say,

throwing open a door, a window, folding back
bedclothes, or hanging blankets out in the garden
in the sun *to air,* so they could live the way

they were meant to. Now, when blood is fired
by the first true sunny day of spring, my students—
like birds feeling the migratory buzz

in their airy bones—shed their clothes like leaves
and flop themselves headlong down on the winter-
scarred remnants of grass, and adore their own

overgod, faces all eager to be lit and filled
by heat, riddled by light, while one last low
mound of snow dwindles minute by minute,

from which I scoop a handful and walk
with its chill reminder, squeezing snow to ice, ice
to freezing water, taking the last bit—big

as a plum but no plum-sweetness to it—
into my mouth, making my teeth ache as I
eat the end of winter, and swallow it down.

New Poems 2006–2008

Window

Sleek blades of rain. Through the window
wind-shriven fuchsia twigs
won't stop shivering. Light, its escalations
and retreats: quickened limb-shapes
fling themselves into the willing curtains.
A naked lemon: waxy skin-gleam
leading its corruscating, bitter life
on the window-ledge. And one orange
lighting up my writing table—resurrected
like a single square inch of a Caravaggio
by the sudden sun-shaft calling it to awe, half
its incandescent, sweet-stocked globe in shadow.

Touch

Surely it's for the comfort of touch (just as we two through the night
let our sleeping hands rest along each other's flesh, warming them),

that these two ruffle-winged, orange-breasted robins nudge each other
through air above a dead-bough birch before settling, all skittery life,

among rotted branches, then steady themselves to preen and look about
for maybe a minute, then take off, lighting out one after the other into that

wide aloneness that has to be their normal life, flying from sight, separate
but heading in the same direction (*traversing,* says Traherne, *the regions*

of air), every wing-beat a quick-tilting, intimate adjustment to the necessary
perfection of flight, just as our sleeping hands take stock of how our bodies

shift through the small hours, adjusting to whatever (in the touch and go
of time and circumstance) passes for perfection in the way of two being

simply together, just as this pair of robins simply part the air between them
in their above-earth hurry—each alone, attending, knowing the other there.

Dublin-Poughkeepsie: Bread Knife in Exile

Home from home again, the song of my mother's bread knife
stops me mid-slice, teeth of Sheffield steel making their own music
that'd cut through the cackle and half-truths of our first kitchen
as she'd sever the black crust of an elbow turnover
or slice into the burnt brown of the Vienna roll
she'd slather with country butter, its salty sweat
making our mouths water where we stood in the light
of the world as was that has become the here and now
of the world as is: a few streaks of sunlight bringing in
fall flicker and stipple-shadow, leaves turning
amber, ginger, rust as the season beyond the window turns
and I settle a migrant heart again in this otherwhere,
hearing the persistent shrill stitching of one late September cricket,
which my mother, though only a ghost, cocks her one good ear to,
stopping the bread knife mid-slice to listen, stunned
to silence first, then turning to ask me what that strange insect
singing is—but before I can answer she's smiling anyway, saying
yes in her old way to it, to what's becoming, foreign as it is,
familiar as the music her bone-handled bread knife goes on making,
which long ago, now, and far away, she stopped noticing.

In the Kitchen with Yeats

> *A poet never speaks directly as to someone*
> *at the breakfast table . . . even when [he] seems*
> *most himself, he is never the bundle of accident*
> *and incoherence that sits down to breakfast.*
>
> (W. B. YEATS)

Since the poet is never the man
that sits down to breakfast,
never that bundle of bits and pieces
but the composed whole bloke
buzzing iambics behind a closed door,
I suppose he wasn't one to linger
if ever he visited the kitchen—
his sense of smell confined
to incense, honey, wine
and other emblematic fragrances.
So what would he make of me
in this cottage kitchen on his birthday
stirring a sauce for pasta, one hand
holding a wooden spoon, the other
his *Collected Poems,* a fresh edition?

With one ear I listen
to the homely little splutter
of tomatoes, spices, garlic, a diced onion
as they bubble
towards their unity of being,
while with the other I can hear
the clear, austere music
of "The Wild Swans at Coole,"
the ache of its defeats beating
through that one lost rhyme each stanza,
and through those clean lifelines of his
that keep cheating us out of ease
but lead to grace. Wooden spoon

tapping the skillet, I close my eyes
to get the poem by heart, making
its cold companionable manners
my own as long as that music lasts,
while all the while the cottage
fills to steamy brimming
with smells that distill into the air
some vegetarian notion of the soul,
and fills with the ceremony of sound
he stirred into the stock
of his own marrowbone soup—
to keep us, even in lean times,
warm. Now, when I close the book
and leave the sauce to simmer,

the whole place breathes
a single compound smell
of garlic tomatoes onions oregano
pepper cinnamon wild thyme all
in a base of olive oil and crowned
with a leaf or two of bay. Later—
wondering how he might have relished
the scent of his own ascending dinner
winding up the winding stairs—
I'll spoon the wine-dark mixture
over *fettuccine,* sprinkle parmesan
(aged nine months), prop up
his book against the bowl, and eat.

Oh, This and That

... of such stuff is the world about them

(KEATS, LETTER, 24 APRIL, 1818)

From their perches on rock or branch, drenched robins, blackbirds, wrens peer out perplexed at the pock-marked pools that, along with the electric green of grass, are the only bright spots in a world given over to spongy cloud and a steady slow downpour of rain. Into a casket made of wax paper and tape, I'm pressing three flowers of blood-tinted fuchsia. A sun-stamped world away, in the stricken marketplace, blood is drying on the shattered steering column of one exploded Volkswagen. Among the terrorised scattershots of lemons, cantaloupes, dates and figs, blood-boltered fragments of cheekbone, bits of brain tissue, flutters an amber and emerald headscarf, dangles a sandal with foot attached: everything—including the charred rainbow wings of a cageful of singing-birds—*in flagrante* under a sun you'd hardly see for smoke. And here, on the shine of the skylight, rain plays its steady, finger-drumming dirge, while at intervals a single wheezy robin is making this terrible world, against the odds, musical.

The System

Two flies flicker-fucking on a dollop of gullshit
near navy-blue waves scouring the packed sand
will hardly make a meal for the few remaining swallows

who twitter under cloud-clusters shading the azure
of a sky washed overnight by weltering rain
in air trailing tail-wise off Hurricane Gordon

that's spent most of its force over the Atlantic—
as liver-brown mounds of kelp on the White Strand
tell us. Or they may be—these same flies shaking

their little shiver-timbers in a single sex-frenzy—
a sign of something: of that ineradicable drive
that aligns, so the poet tells us, *love's mansion*

with *the place of excrement.* No matter. I keep
close watch till they've done buzzing and skive off
in different directions: one over the tonguing waves

towards Mayo, the other aiming—on a lightly
auspicious, fly-pleasing breeze—for the near field,
where the last of the last of the swallows is waiting.

Going Back

> *What would it be to be water,*
> *one body of water . . .*
> —MARIE PONSOT, "SPRINGING"

What if a going back to water
were the chosen way?
To immerse: let limb by limb,
appendage, member, drift
to fluency, a permeable,
positive transparency:
to lose all alphabets
and other perturbations
for the pure lap and slither,
the very *oh!* sloth of
simple drift, be nothing
but a boneless, see-through,
barely swimming unicell
before anything, all agog
and afloat in a wordless
soup of sensory (sort of)
cognitives, dead set
on the staying power
of the mere glitter
of being itself, perdurable
and simple, till live liquid
gives up even the last ghost
of the ghost of a last chance
of becoming anything
but a bubble of light
with all the action
of the wide world captured
in its spectral glimmer-sphere
of rainbows, its constellation
of radiant ache, a truly new
beyond-all-known-elements

unspoken universe
holding an almost readable sign
haloed over what
you'd take for an entryway,
seeing words
in one of the tongues
you've cut yourself off from—
spelling out *it's white, white . . .*
a heart-jet, a river . . .
so you'll start over again
as if you'd never felt
at home on earth's
solidity, nor even there
where a new succesion
sings and flies—
beyond question
or appetite
or expectation.

Blind Road Blues

From bed-warm flesh to rainy daylight seeping through pink curtains you wake to stare another death in the face, stumble bluntly into furniture, start the stunned debate with the face gaping back from the pitiless mirror, dictating the hundred and one questions. Outside, sharp magpie eyes on fire for the first crumb of morning. Thin-as-filament insects scuttling from the paint brush; terror of the black-back spider disturbed from dungy slumber by footsteps on its inch of gravel: all the passing kinetic quick of the world at the edge of touch as a single breath is taken, let go: death of hundreds, hundreds more wriggling into life. In the big world, the workaday commuters shuffle on to world's end through the mortared bricks of a mortal city: deaf and dumb, they fumble along any blind road, hands held up for a minute's silence in which as on a grim, inky stream the dead flow back with remorseless tidings, ravenous in their unabashed to and fro, their local wan-light hither and thithering—*shameful and vibrant* as any flesh-memory holding its own against the odds and never harvested.

Conflagration Revisited

Ce monde n'est que la crête
d'un invisible incendie.
—PHILIPPE JACCOTTET, *AIRS*

That the leaves are all gone but for a few
gold leftovers clinging to willows, and the oak
only a scuffed chestful of dry browns
rattling at every breeze, may help him remember
how she opened once like a book
learned page after page by heart
as if nothing else mattered: eyes in flight
flung headlong into every hard fact
until all was conflagration, the tip of things
a world of hot tongues whispering *grace-this, grace-that*
as if it meant something, meant he'd come upon
a destination unplanned but recognised
as what he'd been after—a place where
after the ignition of bodies
there was no remainder, where even soul
seemed possible, was not just smoke.

The Day That's in It

The singer with Mozart in her mouth; wind
omnipresent, omniactive as air around the usual:
green lettuce steeped in oil; tang of mashed tomatoes;
plush, full-mouthed, yellowgreen chunks
of avocado; a greywhite gull, cloud-gobbled,
vanishing; invisible windbreath nibbling at
sycamore leaves that shy this way, that; a few
itinerant bees in and out of the fuchsias; wind-
tipped sally leaves shifting green to silver grey;
one dumbstruck bunch of cows stockstill
in their collective gawk of curiosity; blood-boltered
bits of a child and its young mother
flying from the roadside where a bomb
by accident and bad design found them, ending
the day and everything. Still bees patrol the hedges
and one willow warbler lights on a furze bush
to sing its territorial heart out; and still
you can't help looking up to the flash
a gull makes, tilting into the blue where the lark
that started its manic aria minutes ago
is still on fire with it, letting everything go
in one small, ferocious mouthful of music.

World As Is

Between the old stone man in his limestone greatcoat
and the small white house on the hill; between palegreen waves
and the high notes of the plovers as they arrow away
from the strand and my solid figure striding there; between the foal
sheltering under his mother's flank from the slanting rain
and the blackbird at dusk singing and bringing the fixed stars out
lies what bond, I wonder, as I trudge head down, bent
into the protection of hedges, what *delicate machine* makes its presence
felt in the world of spent tabernacles and rattled nerves
we inhabit? Or is it something in the nature of *the evanescent symmetries*
lets this bee—that has banged against my window
and jackhammered there in raging indignation at the irreversible logic
of the fact of glass—be scooped into the soft dark
of the napkin I've wrapped it in, through which I can feel
what we would call its anger, its despair, still quick to the end
it must sense is happening, till I open the cloth outside
and after a second or two of stillness as daylight
envelops it again it lights out and floats off in the free air,
at one again with what makes simple sense to it: the world
as is: things in their exquisite, absolute, inexpressible
balance: work to be done, direction chosen, anything can happen.

Connemara: The Twelve Pins

Peaks, slopes, humped ridges. Gold-lit groves by early light; smooth, soft-towering grace at evening; high inhuman patience in storm; immense sleeping creatures in calm. Steady, they steady the earth that stretches out from their feet, and are day in day out nothing but their own big steadfast ever-shifting shapes appearing and disappearing in cloud-shawls. Shadow and substance in endless *interinanimation* of each other, they wall me in here in a garden of rough grass and ragged hedges lightened by small birds flickering shadow-like among leaves, or skimming the insect-laden weeds, or sheltering between rose bushes and the old field-stone fence, eyes alive to the moment I'll scatter on gravel the crumbs they'll dab among, a mother first feeding her squeaky young one. As a summer kid in Carraroe, these hills—seen from that southern side—were a great wall of hazy blue, a far-off mystery, a massive namelessness: simply, elementally there. Now—although I know their names in two languages—they still mystify, are still a limit to what in any language words can manage. Are, as Li Po says, *a different world, not of the human kind*—indifferent as the Milky Way, yet altering the world as we know it.

After the One O'Clock News

It would take very little, wouldn't it,
to take that horse in the field across the road—
that mare not wayward at all but tranquil
in the wind-wavering domesticity
of grass, her flank, quartz-white,
nuzzled by her coffee-coloured foal, the two
deftly, attentively grooming each other—
take so little in the shape of a blunt gun
or even a wayward missile
landing near my neighbour's shed
to take the two of them, mother and child,
to the end and way beyond the end
of their invisible tether, remove them
from the loop of daily life in a flash
of hot light, a thundercrash, a blood-sodden
thick pink mist and then nothing, nothing
but the riven peace of Letter Hill
echoing what happened, and a drift of
blueblack smoke curling on the cool breeze
across this roof I've tucked myself under,
and floating off over the bay of Ballinakill,
to be sighted near Derryinver pier
as an indecipherable sign of something
seen from far out at sea, or from the cosy homesteads
of Achill, Inishturk, or Inishbofin?

Border Country

What to make of last night's dream:
bulging suitcase, church pews, genuflections,
soft murmurings of friends and strangers,
all the rites and ripples of familiar action
until one walks by in black,
head bowed, stately pacing,
and I have to leave the building
by the back door? Then
the hedged country opening
under a chop of helicopters
and half the hill blown skywards
suddenly in a thunder of smoke
and broken limestone
and nothing to do but duck down
where the wren and its brother dunnock
are sheltering, wishing myself
small as one or the other
so the eye-level knothole in the sycamore
could be a hiding place
I'll shiver to silence in
till smoke thins
and their mild, shy voices start again
and it's time to come out—all
clear into the clear air—and not
be anymore there
where the bright-frocked, head-scarfed
village women are counting over
and over the bones of their dead
children, the men only sitting and staring.

Hardy's Sky

Blanched to a *wintry sneer:* bleak, cloud-broken, swollen with
wind-shiver, grey-gold with touches of crucifixion and apocalypse,
everything a flight, a fugue, so the small voices of these slate juncos
make music a huddle of refugees might make—bedraggled, bent
under tattered loads, feeling the weather change, air harden,
the taste of things grow *harsh and crude* on their forced march
towards haggard light, towards some poor haven, this endless trek
against weather, fires blossoming from the sky ceiling, the ferocious
thump of air waves pushing them, staggering eardrums, pure dread
bursting in scatterflash and stuttercrack, these terminal fireworks
at odds with all past knowledge. So the beat goes on, no end to it,
and in this Thomas Hardy sky you'd see, had you eyes for it, words
like *numb* and *wasting* inscribed, and *sad* or *dim, drearisome, wan,*
and everything tucked in like a heart in its beating chest of bone
so the whole body thrums with it, beaten through and through by it.

On Edge

(Because)

Because the man on the train seat in front of me
wears a black trilby and is playing very softly
a tenor sax, his body shape swaying in the dark
mirror of the window; because the day has
without my noticing entered suddenly into
the tunnel of night so the lights we pass
are doubled in the dream trouble of the river;
because that brightlit path floating in the dark
is a bridge solid-stepping across water; because
I'm caught like this, speechless, almost thoughtless,
empty of everything except the flicker of
what passes; because it's hard to stay afloat;
because the old style of faith and hope has been
extinguished, so it's difficult to find a point
to pray to or wish on; and because I'm hearing
in the clatter and shake of train wheels the rattle-
tune riff of the *bare forked animal,* I can do nothing
except direct this pulsing of the hapless heart
to the other half of the world—where a young man
is setting off high on hope into the unknown,
his good heart beating with the lovely risk of it,
the mission alive in his mind, and seeing *(Let be!)*
the end of it: the found families around him, all
the lost kids recovered, and he so far from home.

(Words)

Hard to be in a state where the simple words *father, son, child*
cause something at the base of the throat to heat up, cause
a stammer to happen in the right eyelid, some out-of-control
ticking in the nerves to register their dismay, their disarray. So
I won't think of what's in the nature of things out there, up there
in rock and ice and snow, out there in the high places, out there

among the nameless deities who—being so far off—may not
be prayed to. But scraping away on this tuneless fiddle
I find it strange how a story of bird-fights staining snow scarlet
distracts me, the blind and deaf black-cocks going at it
in their short ferocious *now or never,* blood pooling their eyes
so nothing at all can be known except the sharpness of life
happening, happening as one foot and then the booted other
of those trekkers among the high places where no roads are
keep measuring the way, keep beating time to their
return journey, their comeback to where they started, which
is when I'll start breathing again, knowing *father, son, child*
as words to melt in my mouth again, not this chill now stinging it.

(Soulstuff: In Flight)

Watching the propellor of this cumbersome blunt-nosed object
rev and spin, become invisible
but for a faint circle inscribed on air, a sort of shadow
of the speed of light, you wonder
could this be an image of the soul—the speedy real
becoming nothing
but the driving force itself and what follows, the way
we know—when we move at last—
it's there, but where? We're airborne then, and under us
spread the square green fields
of Galway, then the rest of Ireland over in no time
and we're above the slow grey writhing
of the Irish Sea, then the green and pleasant ploughlands
of England are coming up
to meet us, sheer speed bearing our load
all the way to where, on a surprise
street in West Hampstead, your son runs up to greet you, a soul
in flight, and finds your shoulders
with his two arms, your two cheeks, astonished, with his kisses.

After Leopardi's *Imitazione*

One fragile, faded leaf.

Where are you off to—

so far from the branch

that bore you? A brisk wind

snatched me

from the ash tree where I was born.

Gusting from the woods

to the open field

it carried me

out of the valley

into the mountains.

A heedless pilgrim now,

I keep wandering about with it.

I go where everything goes:

where the rose-leaf

goes by nature,

and the leaf of the laurel tree.

Out Takes

1.

Searching for some *heart-bright future*
the wren's a furtive quickness, a brown
shadow-scurry among leafshades,
following its beak to some unknown
unpredictable end in this drugged day-stillness
in which the bird—under the immense
certainty of the mountain—goes hunting,
forever a venturing, headlong, impossible-to-stop
flicker in the outcropping rock pile,
risking (little troglodyte) this ceaseless
winding through and through, wherever
the chartless no-road takes it.

2.

How slow they are
to let their one and only last attachment
to rock or weed or fellow creature
go, these mussels wrenched from
salty sleep, prised from the dark
in which they've led their quiet
tide-rocked lives—like any dreamer
on the verge of who knows what
active bliss or passion, but bested
by some half-thought-through
restraint, so his refrain can't help
but be, as he wakes, that sea-blue
see-through mantra: *Loss is nothing*
but more to come. Wailing
daylight, then, and no two ways
about it: detachment happens.

3.

Where you live, ditches brim with
meadowsweet, loosestrife, montbretia,
fugitive dog daisies, forget-me-nots,
the washed purple glow of heather—
and one cow moon-stares
over the fence at your staring self
while among the rushes
six heifers lie in wait for rain:
when it starts to fall they'll slowly
rise—crooking their knees, putting
solid glum foreheads to the ground—
fashioning one of their shapes for prayer.

4.

Steady low rumble-drone of a plane
into Newburgh Airport. Saxophone yawp
of one Canada goose heading south,
its music the squeak of unoiled pedals
on the bike I'd cycle up Clareville Road,
last-gasping the last mile home.
Not to mention sunshine
flattening itself against a redbrick wall
in *The View of Delft:* a square
of the immaculate fallen light of the world
coming to immortal terms
with mortal stone, casting solid shadows.

Prayer

Peace means these,
And all things, as before.
—WALLACE STEVENS, "PHASES"

Though I know the settled sound these cows are making
as they trawl among rushes, buttercups and sweet grass
cannot be heard under the rubble of cities, still I can hope
the voices out of my neighbour's radio as they vanish
among fuchsia flowers and the bees humming from
cup to honey-cup might find the hidden way to peace,
bring cease-fire and silence into the shaken world, let
the smoke settle and the people go indoors again, pick up
their dinner things, fill the glass jugs with water, the flowered
plates with food, taste the olives again, the oranges
and dates, the roast lamb on its bed of yellow rice,
and call down out of nowhere the usual blessings on the food
and the feasters—with no more than the racket of traffic
or the jubilant ramshackle neighbourhood chatter or
the rusty tinkle of goatbells out in the world to disturb them.

Interior with Peering Girl

World as is a cracked looking-glass. Stormwinds playing havoc with the garden. A young birch glassy with rain is a tattered sail in the wind. Never not hell to pay, you think, for one compact body stepping along ledges: your head all flirt and provocation for a hazardous, inwit-bitten, sorrowful decade of days, till a fresh thought veers in, hauling a *drift of chosen females in their shifts,* including *that famous milkmaid by Vermeer of Delft, artistic.* You crave a way forward, then, or to be rain-borne, even, over the near hill to the next vantage point, that rocky outcrop deep in the dream interior where, with push come to shove, you might—standing bare—see the future from. Like that girl could, with her close-cropped mind and inquiring eye, who peers over her shoulder at a past tense (greeting it or going away) and may any minute turn, full face, and say something to unsettle you—you and the ground you've taken another firm, half-sober stand on.

Figure

When I shake out the amber tablecloth that covers my writing desk
what comes to mind is not the day-after-day I've spent here
seeing the summer go and this broken autumn bear in behind it,
nor the words marshaled here, the poems read, written, relinquished,

but the figure of a woman in late-summer dusk at her kitchen door,
who stands a minute to take in whatever's happening in the air
around her—clean evening sound of a single yellowhammer,
dense smells the season is fermenting—and who's alive suddenly

to the frantic wreckage of sex: the thought of bodies joined like hands
locked in prayer, a prayer going nowhere, only rebounding back
to bodies that drunk or sober are our only gods, so we adore
their foibles, their hand-to-hand, hard-to-take, ineluctable excesses,

the light of their visible, audible, provisional perfection, or near it.

A Walk on Long Beach Island

Breakers swell and splash. The horizon hillocked by fishing boats hoovering the sea-floor. Before long, herring, bluefish, bass may be words only, entries in those dictionaries of what's no more in this diminishing world we've rioted over, ransacking it. Light cracks to shatterglass on the sea's cobbled surface, and a family of dark-plumed plovers forages among rocks of a breakwater, probing the livid green of sea-washed weed. Five figures—clad head to toe in black—stand upright on the curling surf, lords of water for a minute or two, as the herring gulls must imagine themselves, keeping a doleful yellow weather-eye on things, their hunger unappeasable, no matter how many hand-size grey slitherings of clam they crack into, crying off-key defiant cries to their only god: the quick, all-containing air they inhabit as these butterflies do as they dip to sip sweetness from twisted skinny clumps of goldenrod in dune grass. Turning inland, I stop to watch a couple of gilded flies go to it pell-mell among the rose-red, lethal-to-you-and-me yew berries. How everything is at once, for once: the Atlantic's clear, near-dream metronome marking it.

Apparitions

Death upon death from the radio:
still a robin sweetens air and ash tree
with sleepy music.

Nibbling on fecund cowshit,
these flies the color of ground ginger
belong to an abundant species.

In their parlor of clay
the blood-colored worms
wind themselves like clocks.

But who is that ticking away
in the hydrangeas, brief shadow
flickflickering between leaves?

The wren, stone-born, winging
a frantic tattoo as it spins
about itself intricate leafshade.

The day a braid of shadow-facts
dwindling toward midnight,
when—heart hammering its own

wrenflap fandango—you walk
through the dark of the dark
in a pool of pale lamplight

humming the overture to *Macbeth,*

and cower away from your own kind:
a brace of whisperboys
coming, cowled, against you.

Watch

1.

Watching it closely, respecting its mystery,
is the note you've pinned above the heavy Dutch table
that takes the light weight of what you work at—
coaxing the seen and any unseen it might secrete
into words that mightn't fall too far short, might let you
hear how the hum of bees in the pink fuchsia
and among the buttercups and fat blackberries
is echoed by that deep *shwissshhh*-sound that is
your own blood coursing its steady laps
and speaking in beats to the drum of your left ear.

2.

When you watch the way the sycamore leaf curls,
browns, dries and drops from the branch it's lived on
since spring, to be blown by a soundless breeze
along seed-heads of the uncut grass, then
the mystery that is its movement—the movement,
that is, from seed to leaf-shard and so on
to fructive dust—holds still an instant, gives a glimpse
of something that quickens away from language
into the riddling bustle of just the actual as you
grab at it and it disappears again, again unsaid.

Ergo What

Even Descartes' head
after all his homeless
house-shifting in Holland
went missing. In the grave

he lies beyond *cogito,*
although the rest—that
vacant house of bone—
remains at rest there,

abiding our question now
when we look out
at vines of bittersweet
blazing from bare rock

or at the lithe span
of the Mid-Hudson Bridge
walking tall on water,
so we can in the end

do no more than
propose mystery
as no more than
the way things are

and are seen from this
shifting peninsula, this
headland we have
to stand on, looking out.

Parents and Departing Train

For all the wavering truth of trees reflected in rainwater, or the undulant
disappearing bulk of the white-tail deer into the deer-colored dusk
of the apple orchard, its raised tail a pennant of life on the run, its
pure white glimmer-candle gone as soon as seen; for all that I believe

of transience—each moment murdered by the next one, each breath
dying into its twin—it still seems impossible to find a right language
for how our daughter shoulders her heavy bags and boards the train
and is taken from us, just a shadow of a shadow kissing its fingers

at where our shadows stand outside, me settling an arm around
your shoulders, your pale face and hair nearly ghostly in the air
that's otherwise all gold, saffron, burgundy, rust—as our girl, speedy
as any express—is taken into the distance her own life is now, a place

beyond lullaby or open-eyed angel, a nameless space we keep
peering into for that sheer glimmer, girl-shaped, flickering into dusk.

A Breath of Wind

In the chronicle of the overlooked
try to register again
this big life-giving breath
that never stops gathering light
and spreading it in every direction.
Cloud comes, goes, hauling
its grave weight, letting its
particle-drench tend everything
and be a downhill quickness
baring rocks so they glitter, feeding
tall, blood-letting, blue-headed
thistles, making thin green rushes
glisten in the wind
that here on the very edge of things
can't let you be—so you may go
about and about only, squinting
into what's there and isn't there, all appetite
for any slow explosion of
unearned felicity. Meanwhile
this morning's hare
takes the disheveled garden
in his stride and stops, not a bother on him,
to sniff then delicately nibble
the lettuce leaves that yesterday
the wind and draggle-sheets of rain
were shaking, and that
last night from a scoured sky
all the firefolk sitting in the air
gazed intently down on. And now
in its *spaciousness and light*
this local wind's all exhalation—
gusting southeast, northeast, no telling
what a half-god of earth and air will do—
pushing, rushing, hushing

towards its sole rest, the silence it settles in
along mute grass blades, stilled sycamore leaves,
even among these dead in shaken bundles
at your shut front door,
where it will get its breath back
to bear itself off in a flurry-hurry
and flow away from where you stand
feeling again the way it came unbidden,
so you would close your eyes
for a moment and be in it,
though you'll open them again
under the starless mantle of darkness,
night-walking home alone after midnight
and knowing the gale's full brunt and buffet
with rain in its teeth, its burly
unavailing out-breath like a last love-gasp
through the pine grove and no holding it.

Quick

When I saw the rainbow shine to life from the flank of Letter Hill
and stand like a ladder of magic and hang there, half-formed,

and beheld the wren fussing among fuchsia twigs in fierce pursuit of flies
and snapping at every shadow, I thought I'd been blessed enough

by quickness and colour for one morning, till I stumbled
across the dead hare, one quick thing stilled where the car had hit and

left it as Chardin might have offered it up to us, or Chaim Soutine
have laid it naked to our gaze in its slicked-back, blood-spotted

brown coat, its back legs acutely angled, a dash of white
under each front paw, one clouded grey eye open on nothing—

in the infinite depths of which that rainbow reflected itself
for a few minutes, maybe, with maybe the occasional bird-shade

flashing on a blank canvas of blue before, in a flash, vanishing.

Ready

Standing motionless in the midst of infinity.
—NAZIM HIKMET

It's a skinny horse he's describing—
a crippled nag outside his cell window—
while he writes another letter to his wife.

I can see it in the stillness, too, in this
grey Connemara mare
whose head droops a little, simply being there

while her foal stares at me
over the hedge, the mother in that moment
being the centre of a world

without borders, in a second so dense
with mere being it throws time into meltdown
and I join the animal in it for a timeless minute

before coming to myself again and walking on
with a headful of Hikmet in prison
who's telling his wife how he faces into silence

by singing *in the thin piping voice of my childhood,*
and how in spring
he's led out to sunshine for the first time

and stands, animal-like, *motionless in wonder,*
and stays emptied out like that and happy,
his back against the wall,

like the birds I've seen
standing stilled for minutes at a time
in the shelter of hedges

and staring out without moving a feather,
eyes full of nothing but emptiness, *entranced*
in every sense, it seems,

by the feel of just being there, the sense
of being anything at all, or nothing,
with no fixed abode but the body—

like a sail, says Hikmet, *ready for the journey.*

From This to That

Stepping overboard from the dream-laden vessel of sleep—
its cargo of foreign tongues, sunsplit stones of Italy, one
coloured bundle of kindlewood, and the music of God knows who
played on the French horn by the poet's only daughter—

you walk awhile by the actual tide-line, the ocean drawn back
to expose sea-rocks colonised by purple-painted tribes
of young mussels, where three oystercatchers grown hysterical
at the frightful sight of you leave their lethal business

among molluscs, to flap-flee over the waves in baffling
blackwhitewhiteblack Escher-flashes. You attend, then,
to the lime-green toupees of weed the near rocks wear, take in
the shore-line glint of scabious and coltsfoot, the quick ignitions

of a few leftover leaves of pink thrift, see one short-masted
black trawler riding the waves, and spot the head
and periscoped neck of a cormorant as it vanishes
between breaths, reappears, and looks about as if surprised

to find the world as is—sky, sea, the rugged bulk of Mweelrea
keeping one from the other—as you yourself look about, minding
the seabird's amphibian gift to live underwater and in air,
to stand on its isolate perch in the wingspread very image

of a black phoenix rising. Stumble on, so, to true wakefulness,
all dreams dissipated, and stop silenced on a seal-smooth rock
half-buried in sand, knowing nothing but the burden
of what you've seen, pondering the simple specific gravity of it,

the jag-line leading from this to that, before you turn for home.

Notes to *New Poems* (2006–2008):

"Going Back": phrases in italics are from, respectively, Paul Celan ("Windmills") and Henry Vaughan ("The Timber").

"World As Is": the phrases in italics are by Wallace Stevens: from, respectively, "Negation" and "Romance for a Demoiselle Lying in Grass."

"Hardy's Sky": the first phrase in italics is from Hardy's poem, "Wessex Heights," and the second from Milton's *Lycidas.*

"Out Takes, 1": the phrase in italics *(heart-bright future)* is Paul Celan's, in "Anabasis" (trans. Michael Hamburger).

"Interior with Peering Girl": the first phrase in italics is from J. M. Synge, *The Playboy of the Western World,* and the second from an early commentator on Dutch art.

"Watch": the phrase in italics is from an essay by Ann Ferry on Elizabeth Bishop called "The Poet of 'The Fish'" in *Tradition and the Individual Poem.*

"A Breath of Wind": the first phrase in italics is from Gerard Manley Hopkins ("The Starlight Night"), and the second from Wallace Stevens ("Anatomy of Melancholy").

Acknowledgements

Grateful acknowledgement is made to the editors of the following magazines, where many of the poems in the *New Poems* (2006–2008) section first appeared (often in somewhat different versions):

Agenda: "Border Country"
An Sionnach: "After the One O'Clock News," "Quick"
Crab Orchard Review: "Out Takes, 3" (as "Landscape with Sacred Cows")
The Florida Review: "Soul Stuff: In Flight"
The Hudson Review: "World As Is," "Prayer"
The Irish Times: "Parents and Departing Train," "Out Takes, 4" (as "Sound, Light, Time, Space")
Lumina: "The System"
The New Republic: "Hardy's Sky"
The New Yorker: "From This to That"
Philoctetes: "Out Takes, 2" (as "Mussel Dreaming")
Poetry Ireland Review: "Out Takes, 1" (as "Wren"), "Dublin-Poughkeepsie: Bread Knife in Exile"
Poetry London: "Ready"
Poetry Northwest: "A Walk on Long Beach Island"
The Same: "Interior with Peering Girl"
The Sewanee Review: "Apparitions"
Slate: "Watch"
Smartish Pace: "After Leopardi's *Imitazione,*" "Window"
Stinging Fly: "Oh, This and That," "Blind Road Blues"
The Threepenny Review: "*Ergo* What"
The Warwick Review: "Touch"
Washington Square: "Because"

"In the Kitchen with Yeats" first appeared in *Facing the Music: Irish Poetry in the Twentieth Century.*

For their unfailing generosity, heartfelt thanks to my family in Ireland, England, and Scotland: Deirdre, Tommy and Anne, and Dermot.

EAMON GRENNAN was born in Dublin, Ireland, in 1941 and has spent over forty years living and working in the United States. An emeritus professor of English at Vassar College, he currently teaches in the graduate creative writing programs at Columbia University and New York University. He is the author of numerous collections of poetry, published both in Ireland and the United States. *Still Life with Waterfall* won the 2003 Lenore Marshall Poetry Prize of the Academy of American Poets. His collection of translations, *Leopardi: Selected Poems,* won the PEN Translation Award for Poetry. His translation (with Rachel Kitzinger) of *Oedipus at Colonus* was published by Oxford University Press in 2005. He has also published a book of criticism, *Facing the Music: Irish Poetry in the Twentieth Century.* He divides his time between Poughkeepsie, New York, and Renvyle, in the West of Ireland.

Book design by Rachel Holscher. Composition by BookMobile Design and Publishing Services, Minneapolis, Minnesota. Manufactured by Maple Vail on acid-free paper.